CHAMBER THEATRE

CHAMBER THEATRE

ROBERT S. BREEN

Northwestern University

PRENTICE-HALL, INC. ENGLEWOOD CLIFFS, N.J. 07632

Library of Congress Cataloging in Publication Data

Breen, Robert S (date).
    Chamber theatre.

    Bibliography: p.
    Includes index.
    1. Chamber theater. I. Title.
PN4148.B7   809.2'5'1   77-6386
ISBN 0-13-125211-9 pbk.

©1978 by Prentice-Hall, Inc., Englewood Cliffs, N.J. 07632

Printed in the United States of America

10 9 8 7 6 5 4 3 2 1

PRENTICE-HALL INTERNATIONAL, INC., *London*
PRENTICE-HALL OF AUSTRALIA PTY. LIMITED, *Sydney*
PRENTICE-HALL OF CANADA, LTD., *Toronto*
PRENTICE-HALL OF INDIA PRIVATE LIMITED, *New Delhi*
PRENTICE-HALL OF JAPAN, INC., *Tokyo*
PRENTICE-HALL OF SOUTHEAST ASIA PTE. LTD., *Singapore*
WHITEHALL BOOKS LIMITED, *Wellington, New Zealand*

For G.B.B.

CONTENTS

1   **INTRODUCTION,** *1*

2   **THE SELF,** *6*

3   **POINT OF VIEW,** *21*

4   **STYLE,** *35*

5   **EPIC THEATRE,** *42*

6   **FILM,** *54*

STAGING CHAMBER THEATRE, *69*

SAMPLE SCRIPTS, *89*

Inpulse, Conrad Aiken, *90*
The Third Prize, A.E. Coppard, *97*
The Bride Comes to Yellow Sky, Stephen Crane, *102*
A Country Love Story, Jean Stafford, *105*
Why I Live at the P.O., Eudora Welty, *108*

BIBLIOGRAPHY, *115*

INDEX , *125*

CHAMBER THEATRE

1
INTRODUCTION

The child's plea, "Tell me a story," is familiar enough, but it might surprise us a little if he or she said, "*Show* me a story." The child is content to have the storyteller use words which when sounded will suggest to the mind images of action, characters, and settings. The youngster does not expect the storyteller to *show* these elements, but is content to be told. However, when this same child goes to the theatre, he or she expects to *see* the story, and not have to *imagine* the action, characters, and settings.

When mature readers meet a story in print, they may say that it *tells* a story of life in a concentration camp or, just as readily, comment that it *shows* how people will act in a concentration camp. Sophisticated readers who meet literature on the printed page do not make any conscious distinction between the story as it appears in cold print and the story as it unfolds before the inner eye and ear. The convention which allows a story to be told in print, at the same time that it is shown in images, does not demand that there be a dominance of the one over the other, or that a satisfactory alternation be established.

Child and adult, alike, are persuaded by the mysterious genius of language, especially in its mimetic and analogic condition, that the art of literature consists in the capacity of language to embody what it indicates. The language of the dramatic mode is more apt to imitate reality,

1

whereas the language of the epic or narrative mode is more apt to indicate reality.[1]

Traditionally, the dramatic mode has been almost synonymous with *showing* a story, while the epic or narrative mode has meant *telling* a story. It is difficult, in the light of actual literary practice, to maintain such a categorical distinction, for dramatists and novelists alike will show *and* tell.

Greek playwrights used messengers to tell their audiences things that had happened "off stage"; Elizabethan dramatists used the convention of the soliloquy to tell characters' thoughts and motives. The use of the confidant in eighteenth-century drama is but a thinly disguised narrative device for telling the audience what a character is thinking or feeling or to relate a scene that has taken place "off stage."

Unlike the dramatist, the novelist has no expectation of literally showing the action of a story. Despite a commitment to *telling* the story, the novelist, nevertheless, subscribes to Conrad's injunction to the writer of fiction to make the reader *see*. Thus the characters in a narrative will speak in dialogue, giving the reader the illusion that they are exercising free will and responding spontaneously to the given circumstances. This use of dramatic elements is enhanced by descriptions of gestures or facial expressions, etc., after the manner of stage directions. Frequently a storyteller will prefer to show a character in action rather than tell the reader what the character's internal condition is. For example, one novelist may prefer to say, "She blushed and lowered her eyes," leaving the reader to conclude from the evidence of her behavior that she was embarrassed. Another, less concerned with making the reader see, will simply say, "She was embarrassed."

Since the novelist, like the dramatist, does indeed both show and tell, it is not unreasonable to suggest that if a drama can be appreciated in printed form where the action must be imagined, then the novel, no less than the play, can be appreciated when staged in the theatre.

However, if a formal distinction between drama and narrative literature is insisted upon, certain aesthetic consequences follow. The drama depends for its vitality and immediacy on the fact that its action develops from the rhythmic interaction of characters. The dramatic value of a play derives in large part from seeing simultaneously the reaction of one character to the action of another. Swordplay on the stage depends for its effectiveness upon seeing the thrust and parry simultaneously, whereas fiction must be content with a serial presentation that sees first

---

[1]Language which indicates, points to, or refers to reality is sometimes called "semantic," whereas language which is adjusted to reality in such a way as to imitate it is called "iconic." See Charles W. Morris, *Signs, Language and Behavior*, New York: George Braziller, 1955. See also Charles W. Morris, "Foundations of a Theory of Signs," *International Encyclopedia of Unified Science*, Vol. 1, no. 2 (Chicago: University of Chicago Press, 1938).

the thrust and then the parry. Such a representation is not quite in the condition of life, but there are compensations. The conventions of fiction will allow the duel to be interrupted by expressions of the internal condition of the combatants. It is possible in fiction to say, "Henry, fearing to wound his opponent, thrust feebly, while John, rejoicing in the test of skills, parried briskly." It is the virtue of fiction that we can learn of the character's motivations or internal conditions *at the moment of action*. The appeal of drama is principally to the outer eye, the appeal of fiction is to the inner eye.

Simultaneity of action, being so much in the condition of life, accounts for a good deal of the appeal that drama has for the theatregoer. The capacity, traditionally granted to fiction, for exploring the motivation of characters at the moment of action attracts the silent reader. These distinctions are of considerable modal significance, yet the similarities shared by the drama and fiction make them sufficiently compatible so that fiction often serves as the source for a drama. The dramatist, in translating the novel into a play, will minimize the fictional descriptions, eliminate the narrator, localize the action, and shorten the time span in observation of the classical unities. These changes are thought necessary because the appeal of the novel is to the *inner* eye and ear while the play must satisfy the *outer* eye and ear.

The translation of the narrative mode into the dramatic mode need not be as radical as we have suggested. Shakespeare in his plays often uses the narrative devices of description and exposition. In *Antony and Cleopatra* he disregards the unity of place and, after the manner of a novelist, sets his scenes "in several parts of the Roman Empire." Before Antony and Cleopatra make their entrance upon the scene at the opening of the play, Philo describes to Demetrius, a surrogate for the audience, the change in Antony's character since he has met Cleopatra. The description is in the tradition of the narrative mode; then at the end of his speech, upon the entrance of Antony and Cleopatra, he says,

> *Look, where they come:*
> *Take but good note, and you shall see in him*
> *The triple pillar of the world transform'd*
> *Into a strumpet's fool: behold and see.*

Shakespeare must tell *and* show. Here the function of the narrator is assumed by the character, Philo, while Antony and Cleopatra conform to the dramatic mode in their dialogical exchange.

The similarities between the novel and the play are sufficiently significant to warrant the recommendation that they share the same means of publication. For the reading public they already do. Plays and novels alike appear in print and are enjoyed by silent readers.

It is the thesis of this text that there is a technique for presenting narrative fiction on the stage in such a way as to take full advantage of all the theatrical devices of the stage without sacrificing the narrative elements of the literature. The technique is called Chamber Theatre. Like chamber music, which explores in intimate fashion the character and quality of a few instruments in harmonic relationships, Chamber Theatre explores the relationships among characters in a narrative context provided by the narrator's intimate association with the audience. This technique was first demonstrated publicly in 1947 at Northwestern University after a series of classroom experiments designed to improve the oral interpretation of fiction. It was some years later that Strindberg's Chamber Plays came to our attention and though they observed the dramatic conventions, we recognized that Strindberg's interest in the close examination of the psychology of a few characters in a small theatre with a close relationship to the audience reflected the same kind of interest that we took in Chamber Theatre.

Since that time Chamber Theatre has demonstrated its capacity to deal with narrative literature more analogous to symphonic structures than to chamber music, for ambitious Chamber Theatre productions of *Moby-Dick, Don Quixote*, and *Anna Karenina* have met with some success. However, after thirty years the term Chamber Theatre has achieved sufficient currency to make changing the name difficult if not inadvisable.

Chamber Theatre is not interested in the problems of transforming fiction into drama; it resists the temptation to delete narrative descriptions and rewrite summaries as dialogue. No effort is made in Chamber Theatre to eliminate the narrative point of view which characterizes fiction; indeed, the storyteller's angle of vision is emphasized through physical representation on the stage.

Chamber Theatre sees virtue in the concept of "simultaneity" and borrows it from drama for the purpose of vivifying and clarifying narrative action. Chamber Theatre also sees virtue in the novel's unique contribution to storytelling, the technique of *exploring motivation at the moment of action*. The lively presentation of characters in action on the stage is appealing, but the playwright runs the risk of oversimplifying his characters since, in the theatre, their *patent* natures must readily express their *latent* natures. In the novel, the narrative technique allows for a more thorough exploration of motivation. Since the *serial* representation of an action is by its very nature *interrupted* representation, it does not distress us when the novelist interrupts at the very moment of action to examine the character's motivation. Such anatomized behavior in the course of atomized action presumably leads to an understanding somewhat richer and fuller than is possible in the hurly-burly of simultaneous action. While the play is more "in the condition of life," the novel provides a better opportunity for that "intransitive attention" which characterizes the aesthetic experience.

Chamber Theatre recognizes that the drama has never entirely abandoned its narrative devices: messengers, choruses, soliloquies, asides, confidants. In contemporary drama, playwrights like Thornton Wilder, Tennessee Williams, Edward Albee, and others have made explicit use of narrators in their plays.

Chamber Theatre appreciates, too, that fiction has, in the course of its brief history, grown increasingly reliant on dramatic action and dialogue in the development of its characteristic structure. Novelists like William Faulkner, James Joyce, and John Barth have incorporated into their novels long, uninterrupted passages of dramatic dialogue and even full-length plays.

Chamber Theatre is dedicated to the proposition that the ideal literary experience is one in which the simultaneity of the drama, representing the illusion of actuality (that is, social and psychological realism), may be profitably combined with the novel's narrative privilege of examining human motivation at the moment of action.

2
SELF

Chamber Theatre is a *technique*, not an art. It lacks the creative autonomy of art; rather it provides a practical and formal means by which the art of literature may be manifested. Chamber Theatre is in the service of literature; it makes manifest for an audience the structure, the theme, and the tone of literature. Chamber Theatre articulates the literary elements directly; the literature itself is always in focus, always present while the Chamber Theatre performance is in progress.

It is not difficult to imagine how the technique of staging a traditional novel would succeed in presenting the action of characters in a setting—structural elements which fiction shares with the drama. It is more difficult to imagine how the novels of certain modern writers might be served by the technique of Chamber Theatre because they seem to lack the traditional concern for plot, character, and setting. And yet Chamber Theatre has successfully staged them. Writers like Kafka, Joyce, Beckett, Sartre, and Nabokov create novels in which much of the action takes place on the *inner* stage of the characters' minds; the traditional conflicts are not socialized as in the "boy-meets-girl" dramas, but tend to be psychologized.

Much of modern literature is concerned with the self, the threat of fragmentation of reality which creates anxiety. Modern man is anxious, in retreat, seeking certainty in himself, only to discover that he does not know himself. His introspective monologues cut him off from communication with others. Nevertheless, he must strive to know; despite uncertainty, he must seek the light of self-knowledge.

As long as the introspective monologues remain monologues they will be treated on the stage as soliloquies addressed to the audience. But if it can be shown that such monologues are actually dialogues we have the option of externalizing these inner conflicts in dramatic form rather than presenting them lyrically as traditional soliloguies. Before we attempt to state these psychic dialogues we must examine their nature more fully.

It is possible, still, to speak of self-knowledge as the highest aim of philosophical inquiry. For Socrates the important question was "What is man?" The important imperative for Socrates was "Know thyself!" Whatever the answer to the question was to be, Socrates expected it to be rational. A serious response to the imperative was a response to oneself and to others. A serious consideration of the question and a serious response to the injunction would entail the individual's becoming a "responsible" being, a moral subject.[1] This self-questioning was dialogical and Plato dramatized Socrates's inquiries in the form of dialogues.

The modern equivalent of Socrates's dialogical search for the inner truth is found in Jung's recommendation that every man or woman develop the capacity for holding conversations with his or her own unconscious, his anima, her animus. Jung believed that men and women should learn to put questions to their psyches, treat them as distinct personalities with voices of their own. Such a recommendation may seem intellectually and rationally ridiculous, but if we learn to regard the expressions of the psyche as objectively as we do our dreams, and refuse to take responsibility for them, we can discourse with our psyche as freely as the primitive Negro discourses with his "snake." Jung says:

> . . . one should cultivate the art of conversing with oneself in the setting provided by an affect, as though the affect itself were speaking without regard to our rational criticism. So long as the affect is speaking, criticism should be withheld. But once it has presented its case we should begin criticizing as conscientiously as though a real person closely connected with us were our interlocutor.[2]

For Socrates the process of self-questioning is a rational process; for Jung it is first irrational, affective, spontaneous, and familiar—only later does it become a rational, critical evaluation.

It is not surprising to learn that prisoners often develop the knack of talking to themselves in internal dialogues. Driven in on themselves by

---

[1] Ernst Cassirer, *An Essay on Man* (New York: Doubleday Anchor Books, 1953), p. 21.

[2] Carl G. Jung, "Two Essays on Analytical Psychology" in *Collected Works of C. G. Jung*, Vol 7 (London: Routledge & Kegan Paul, Ltd., 1953), p. 201. Reprinted with the permission of the publishers.

the isolation, they discover that the thought processes once regarded as interior monologues are in fact dialogues. Peter Moen, in his diary written during his internment in a concentration camp, shows how, within a short while, the need for inner dialogue develops, and the extent to which the self is bifurcated. On page two of his diary he notes that "the trial of the inner self is very painful."[3] On page ten Moen speaks of himself objectively—"You will be shot." By the fifteenth page he has clearly established a dialogical relationship with himself—"Peter Moen—can you stand this? Yes, I can—with God's help I *will* hold out," and again on page seventeen:

> I am on the verge of saying to myself: Now is the day of Atonement. You had to come here to come to yourself. Now bow down in silence and do not complain. But this would be pure rhetoric. I *must* voice my distress.[4]

These dialogues are not to be thought of as mystic in any way; indeed, "they are of a very concrete character and the components are thoroughly tangible," as Rubashov, the central character in Arthur Koestler's novel, *Darkness at Noon*, discovered during his term in prison. He discovered that these dialogues were of a special kind: "dialogues in which one partner remains silent while the other, against all grammatical rules, addresses him as 'I' instead of 'you.' "[5] It is a feature of this experience that the silent partner will, after a period of time, speak in a voice that is at first unfamiliar to the earlier speaker and he may find, as Rubashov did, that his own lips are moving.

The dialogical character of Moen's and Rubashov's internal communion is evident, but frequently we are unaware of the interacting elements, because the form of the inner conversation is thoroughly conventional. In Katherine Anne Porter's story, "Flowering Judas," the casual reader might easily miss the dialogical nature of Laura's inner drama when:

> *She tells herself* that throwing the flower was a mistake, for she is twenty-two years old and knows better; but she refuses to regret it, and *persuades herself* that her negation of all external events as they occur is a sign that she is *gradually perfecting* herself in the

---

[3] Peter Moen, *Peter Moen's Diary* (New York: Creative Age Press, 1951). Reprinted with the permission of Farrar, Straus, & Giroux, Inc. and J. W. Cappelens Forlag.

[4] *Ibid.*, p. 17.

[5] Arthur Koestler, *Darkness at Noon* (New York: Modern Library, 1941), p. 108. Reprinted by permission of Macmillan Publishing Company.

stoicism she strives to cultivate against that disaster she fears, though she cannot name it.[6] [Italics mine.]

At the risk of being premature with an application of Chamber Theatre techniques to a complex internal relationship briefly represented here, we might stage Laura's internal dialogue in this fashion: Laura One represents the Laura who is drawn to the culture and character of the Mexican revolutionaries; Laura Two represents the Laura who admits to being an alien in this country and recognizes the disparity between her values and those of the natives around her. The scene finds Laura One and Laura Two (represented by two actresses) standing at the window of their room looking down on a young lad in the street who is serenading them. On an impulse Laura One throws the lad a flower; the following dialogue ensues:

L. TWO: (*addressing Laura One*) She tells herself that throwing the flower was a mistake, for she is twenty-two years old and knows better;

L. ONE: (*addressing Laura Two*) but she refuses to regret it, and persuades herself that her negation of all external events as they occur is a sign that she is gradually perfecting herself in the stoicism she strives to cultivate against that disaster she fears,

L. TWO: (*finishing the sentence Laura One seems reluctant to finish*) though she cannot name it.

L. ONE: (*admitting the final terror which is that the fear is nameless, she repeats*) though she cannot name it.

The justification for retaining the third person locution of the story in the staged presentation will have to wait for Chapter Five. The repetition of the concluding phrase is a modest interpretative liberty taken by the adaptor.

One of the most talkative lonely women in literature is Edna Earle in Eudora Welty's novel, *The Ponder Heart.* Edna is given to telling long stories in which she refers to herself in the first person, the second person, and sometimes in the third person. She will hold conversations with herself as in this brief passage: "I said, Edna Earle, you'd better get on out of there. All right, I said, but let me get one bath." Such divisions within the self, however idiosyncratic, are not uncommon.

Primitive man was generally awed by those phenomena that appeared to be dissociations of the self. He regarded twins as a violent

---

[6]Katherine Anne Porter, "Flowering Judas," in *Short Story Masterpieces*, eds. Robert Penn Warren and Albert Erskine (New York: Dell Publishing Co., 1954), pp. 384-397. Reprinted by permission of Harcourt Brace Jovanovich, Inc.

demonstration of the disunion of a soul or spirit. He saw something mysterious and evil in his shadow, this thing that was at once his and not his. These sinister aspects of the Double which one finds in Dostoyevsky's *The Double,* Conrad's *The Secret Sharer,* and, of course, Stevenson's "Doctor Jekyll and Mr. Hyde," dramatize, in serious terms, the struggle between the self which is socially admirable and the suppressed or disguised anarchic self. It took civilized man to begin to sense the Double as a comic image. *The Menaechmi, The Comedy of Errors,* and *The Boys from Syracuse* testify to the strength of the comic appeal of mistaken identity.

A common device in literature for creating the impression of a "double" is the mirror, usually a genuine mirror, but often it is a lake or other body of water that reflects the image. The mirror functions very well in creating the illusion of a "double" because it is a device with which we are all familiar and yet we respond with interest to the experience of seeing ourselves in it. Dorothy Richardson, a pioneer of the stream-of-consciousness novel, lets us know what her heroine, Miriam, looks like by having her sit before a mirror. The clear objectification of Miriam's appearance stands in strong contrast to the interest the novel takes in Miriam's interior life. In Tolstoi's novel, *Anna Karenina,* the heroine looks into a mirror late in the story, not to see herself, but to see *into* herself, to examine her soul. In Katherine Mansfield's "The Garden Party," the young girl puts on her mother's hat and seeing herself in a mirror sees herself transformed in such a way as to reveal the nature of certain feelings she has heretofore only vaguely sensed. In Elizabeth Bowen's "The Demon Lover," the principal character is psychologically disturbed and is about to experience her first hallucination when she sees herself in a mirror and the narrator says, "She was confronted by a woman of forty-four." This way of putting the recognition makes it clear that Mrs. Drover sees herself from a dissociated point of view, as though she were looking at someone she did not recognize. The role of the mirror in these cases is essentially mechanical, reflecting simply what the character sees, whether the character's image is subjective or objective.

The mirror is sometimes thought by the novelist to have a quality all its own, independent of the "inlooker's" interpretation. The Marquis de Sade, in *Justine,* says,

> The mirror sees the man as beautiful, the mirror loves the man; another mirror sees the man as frightful and hates him; and it is always the same being who produces the impressions.

If this view of the mirror seems too fanciful, it must be remembered in all charity that neither physiology, nor geometry, nor the laws of optics have explained the processes of perception. Merleau-Ponty, a conscientious observer, denies that a person first sees his or her image *in* a mirror; he prefers the word *through*. It is only later that the individual accounts for the mirror phenomenon by constructing a geometrical representation of it.[7]

Paul Schilder has devised a simple experiment which demonstrates that there is a genuine community in the field of perception between the body-image and the body itself:

> I sit about ten feet away from a mirror holding a pipe or pencil in my hand and look into the mirror. I press my fingers tightly against the pipe and have a clear-cut feeling of pressure in my fingers. When I look intently at the picture of my hand in the mirror I now feel clearly that the sensation of pressure is not only in my fingers in my own hand, but also in the hand which is twenty feet distant in the mirror. . . . This feeling is therefore not only in my actual hand but also in the hand in the mirror. One could say that the postural model of the body is also present in my picture in the mirror. Not only is it the optic picture but it also carries with it tactile sensation.[8]

It must be understood that the experience Schilder describes is not a projection, but an experience as immediate and original as the experience in the real hand. When Schilder describes the hand in the mirror as being "twenty feet distant," though he himself is sitting but ten feet from the mirror, he confirms Merleau-Ponty's contention that human beings first experience their image "through" the mirror.

Chamber Theatre may take advantage of the "mirror" convention to express an objective description of a character even though the mirror is not physically present in the scene. The narrator may assume a position vis-à-vis the character described and speak the narrative description. This staging may serve to create the impression that the character is actually seeing him or herself *as though* facing a mirror. Another possibility would be to have a cheval glass frame on stage (no glass, just the empty frame), and to have the character stand close to the mirror on one side and the narrator equally close to the mirror on the other while the latter describes something close up, like an unruly moustache. Then the character might move back from the mirror to get a fuller view of himself while the narrator moves back a similar distance saying perhaps, "his figure was no longer trim." This interpretation of the mirror image takes advantage of the psychological impression that the character sees himself

---

[7]Maurice Merleau-Ponty, *The Structure of Behavior* (Boston: Beacon Press, 1963), p. 218.

[8]Paul Schilder, *The Image and Appearance of the Human Body* (New York: International Universities Press, 1950), pp. 223-224.

through the mirror rather than *in* the mirror. As a consequence there is a dynamic rather than static relationship between the narrator and the character.

Though we are anticipating our discussion of film techniques in Chapter Six, it might be of value here to suggest how the staging of mirror scenes can take advantage of film conventions. A close-up of the mirror image on film and the close-up of the character whose face is reflected in the mirror are projected on the silver screen of the movie theatre so that the audience is facing both of them alternately without moving from its seats.

On the stage, Chamber Theatre would eliminate the cut from mirror image to character's face by having the narrator and the character face the audience simultaneously. The audience would, without moving, see both the mirror image and the character's face *at once*. The intensity of the moment is increased by the simultaneity of the revelation. One has only to think of Picasso's famous painting of The Girl in the Mirror, in which we see at once both the profile and the full-face of the girl as well as a simultaneous revelation of her and her mirror image, to appreciate the value of the simultaneity in the Chamber Theatre staging.

The optic and tactile impressions one gets from mirror images provide a base for empathic experiences of an emotional nature. We understand the emotional condition of ourselves and others by perceiving the body-image as an expression of personality. Just as Schilder experienced his own body through the mirror image so do we experience the bodies, emotions, and personalities of others through what might by extension be called a "mirror reflection."

Schilder says in the closing pages of his book:

> We may take parts of the bodies of others and incorporate them in our own body-image. This is called appersonization. But we also play completely the role of others, identify ourselves with them, and this may lead to a particular attention and attitude toward parts of our own body.[9]

There is more than a hint of Schilder's view in *Light in August* when Faulkner describes Hightower's source of insights as being a recognition that other people are "simply mirrors in which he watches himself."[10]

The reciprocal influence of the mirrored image and the object so mirrored leads to a complex social life in which the reflected body-images form the primary data of adjustment and understanding. Add to

[9]*Ibid.*, p. 299.
[10]Olga W. Vickery, *The Novels of William Faulkner* (Baton Rouge: Louisiana State University Press, 1959), p. 67.

the *inter*personal relationships of body-images the complex *intra*personal exchanges between mirrored selves within the individual, and we have a basis for understanding the enormous importance of the mirror as a device in literature.

The whole context of literature as an art can be placed in a mirror, the mirror held up to nature. Such a mirror is not a simple reflector devoted to verisimilitude in its presentation of exterior form. The mirror which literature holds up to nature is not only looked *at*, but looked *through*. To see through a mirror there must be illumination from the lamp within the viewer so that he or she actually becomes a participant in the story by virtue of empathic identification. What the eye of art sees in the mirror depends alike on the nature of the seeing eye and the nature of the object seen. In any case, the lamp of inner light modifies the contours of outer form so that we insist that the distortion or interpretation is in the glass.

In narrative forms of literature the distortions of refracted nature are prized for their value in establishing a perspective which is individual, perhaps unique. In dramatic literature destined for the illusionistic or realistic theatre we tolerate a minimum of distortion and encourage a maximum of direct apprehension of reality. We understand, of course, that the direct apprehension is an illusion, but we insist on being persuaded by it.

The function of Chamber Theatre is to use the art of the theatre and all its theatrical devices which encourage the illusion of direct apprehension in order to reflect "the sort of world which mirrors itself," the world which has already been distorted by the narrative point of view. In short, Chamber Theatre holds an undistorted mirror up to an image of the world which the point of view of the narrator has already distorted in his or her individual glass. "Distortion" is used here to refer to those modifications of life which characterize art. Life must be shaped and reshaped before meaning can be clearly apprehended. As Wallace A. Bacon says: "The choice of a point of view is central to the particular modification of experience achieved by any work of art."[11]

Admittedly, the use of the mirror metaphor in literature as a means of dramatizing the "alienation" of the conflicting selves of the protagonist is legion. But so is the use of characters whose substantial presence serves to "mirror" the antagonistic or destructive elements of the self. Chamber Theatre gives substance to the mirror images, as will be seen in the staging of Conrad Aiken's "Impulse" in Chapter Eight, as well as to those characters who represent the shadow, the alter ego, or

[11]Wallace A. Bacon and Robert S. Breen, *Literature as Experience* (New York: McGraw-Hill, 1959), p. 81. Reprinted by permission of the publishers.

the "double" of the protagonist. The obvious technique available to Chamber Theatre is the use of two actors, one to play the role of the protagonist and one to play his mirrored opposite. In his psychoanalytic study of the double in literature Robert Rogers shows that much of what appears to be *inter*character conflict in literature can be seen as *intra*character conflict—the human mind at odds with itself.[12]

In Dostoyevsky's novel, *The Double*,[13] Golyadkin, a self-effacing, petty official, is projected by "some mysterious brazen impulse" into a ballroom where he has not been invited. He is ejected from the party and wanders about the streets. By chance, he meets someone who looks exactly like himself, his Double. The Double appears at Golyadkin's office the next day where he behaves mischievously and ridicules Golyadkin. Obviously Dostoyevsky intended Golyadkin II to be an hallucination representing the assertive, shameless impulses that first propelled Golyadkin I into the ballroom, since the novel ends with the Double propelling him again into the same ballroom.

A Chamber Theatre presentation of *The Double* would, no doubt, use two actors in the roles of Golyadkin I and Golyadkin II. It would be unnecessary and, indeed, inadvisable for the two actors to resemble each other or to be dressed alike. Though they are mirror images of each other, they are, like mirror images, reversed: Golyadkin I is weak, self-effacing, socially incompetent, whereas Golyadkin II is aggressive, shameless, and extrovertive. It is in the interest of creating an "epic alienation" (see Chapter Five), wherein the familiar is made to seem strange, that Golyadkin II, an hallucination, though resembling Golyadkin I, should differ from him in character and appearance. The audience "sees" the differences between the Golyadkins, by insisting on the fundamental identity of the two. There is little chance of the audience being confused to the point of misunderstanding because the narrator is presnet to set them straight:

> Sitting opposite was . . . Mr. Golyadkin himself; not who was now sitting on his chair. . . . No. This was a different Mr. Golyadkin, quite different but at the same time identical with the first—the same height, same build, dressed the same . . . in short the resemblance was perfect. . . .[14]

Dostoyevsky skillfully employs the mirror metaphor without insisting on a reflected likeness:

[12]Robert Rogers, *A Psychoanalytic Study of the Double in Literature* (Detroit: Wayne State University Press, 1970).

[13]Fyodor Dostoyevsky, *The Double*, (Bloomington: Indiana University Press, 1958).

[14]*Ibid.*, p. 89.

Standing in the doorway of the next room . . . which till then he had taken to be a mirror—was a little man. It was Mr. Golyadkin, not Golyadkin the elder, the hero of our tale, but the other, the new Golyadkin. . . .[15]

Autoscopic experiments on the perception of one's own face and body when one's eyes are closed, suggest that "the individual translates himself somehow into the role of the outside observer who sees the person from the front."[16] Golyadkin suffered a pathological hallucination, but Schilder points out that normally

. . . we not only see our own body in the same way as we see outside objects, but we also represent our own body as we represent an outside object. . . . For this purpose, we create a mental point of observation opposite ourselves and outside ourselves and observe ourselves as if we were observing another person.[17]

A Chamber Theatre staging of *The Double* should give us an opportunity to share with Golyadkin I the vivid experience of observing ourselves in just such a manner.

Christopher Isherwood wrote *Down There on a Visit*,[18] an autobiographical novel in four episodes. The dust jacket describes the narrative relationships between the characters:

The "Visitor" who links them [the four episodes] together speaks in the first person and is called by the Author's name. But who, exactly, is he? The twenty-three year old Christopher Isherwood who visits Mr. Lancaster in Germany is not the same Christopher who spends the summer with Ambrose on his Greek island . . . five years later.[19]

Nor is he the same as the third and fourth Christophers. "All these four Christophers are observed by a fifth, the middle-aged Author." The following passage from the novel will illustrate the value of the mirror as a means of dramatizing the fact that memory is always in the present. The middle-aged Author is speaking in the first person of an experience he had at the age of twenty-three while dining with Mr. Lancaster:

Without even telling me to wait for him, Mr. Lancaster fol-

[15]*Ibid.*, p. 145.

[16]Schilder, *The Image and Appearance of the Human Body*, p. 83.

[17]*Ibid.*, p. 84.

[18]*Down There on a Visit* Copyright © 1959, 1961 by Christopher Isherwood. Reprinted by permission of Simon & Schuster, Inc.

[19]*Ibid.*, (see the Dust Jacket)

lowed them [the guests]. I had no alternative but to stay where I was, sitting at the extreme end of one of the settees, facing a large mirror on the wall.

Very very occasionally in the course of your life—goodness knows how or why—a mirror will seem to catch your image and hold it like a camera. Years later, you have only to think of that mirror in order to see yourself just as you appeared in it then. You can even recall the feelings you had as you were looking into it. . . . I know how I looked and felt as I stared into that restaurant mirror.

I see my twenty-three year old face regarding me with large reproachful eyes, from beneath a cowlick of streaky blond hair. . . .

And now I experience what that face is experiencing—the sense which the young so constantly have of being deserted. . . . It isn't that I feel angry with Mr. Lancaster for having deserted me . . . I'm in mortal dread of being challenged by the manager of the restaurant. . . . Suppose they ask me what I'm doing here—why . . . I'm not with the others attending the meeting?[20]

A Chamber Theatre production of this scene from Isherwood's novel would have a young actor in the role of the twenty-three year old Christopher on the settee in the restaurant looking into the mirror (imagined or simply an empty frame) while a middle-aged actor, as the observing Author, looks on and talks to the audience. When the narrator speaks the line, "I see my twenty-three year old face regarding me with reproachful eyes," he places himself in the position of the mirror so that the young Christopher, who is presumably looking into the mirror, is in fact looking into the face of the narrator (his elder self) with reproachful eyes. On the line, "And now I experience what that face is experiencing," the narrator moves to the boy's side of the mirror and sits beside him on the settee. The "now" represents the now of the youth *and* the now of the middle-aged narrator. Earlier, when the narrator says, "I know how I looked and felt as I stared into that restaurant mirror," his use of the past tense suggests that he is speaking from the perspective of memory. When he says, "It isn't that I feel angry with Mr. Lancaster," he is still speaking from the perspective of memory, but his use of the present tense indicates that he is also speaking from the perspective of the boy. There is clearly an ambivalence here—the narrator speaks the line and the boy speaks the line. It is important, then, that the narrator sit beside the boy to share the present moment which is in the restaurant, but at the same time it is the image in the mirror and the feelings that went with it that the narrator is remembering. Perhaps the narrator and the boy could share speaking the lines for the remainder of the passage. It seems right.

In all the episodes of the novel the mirror image is used as a device

---

[20]*Ibid.*, p. 27.

for the narrator's objectification of himself. In the episode that takes place five years later with Ambrose, the middle-aged Christopher comments,

> I seldom thought of Ambrose as a person. Most of the time he was simply a consciousness that was aware of me, a mirror in which I saw my reflection—but dimly, and only if I made big, easily recognizable gestures.[21]

At the opening of the final episode with Paul in California during the forties, the narrator says,

> Another look into the mirror—my own face dimly reflected through a fashionable twilight of a Beverly Hills restaurant, confronting three people on a banquette with their backs to the glass. . . . I don't look happy, and indeed, I am not.[22]

One is reminded, while reading Isherwood's novel, of Auden's remark: "Every man carries with him through life a mirror, as unique and impossible to get rid of as his shadow."[23]

The mirror can be regarded in simple terms as a means whereby "I" get to know "Me." I, the self as knower, gets to know Me, the self as known. William James saw the I and the Me as partners in self-realization. For James, the Me was not only *material* in that it represented a person's body, clothes, house, friends, etc., but it had a *social* constituency made up of the various images of that person that others maintain and a *spiritual* content which James defined as

> . . . the entire collection of my states of consciousness, my mystic faculties and dispositions taken concretely. This collection can at any moment become an object to my thought at that moment and awaken emotions like those awakened by any other portion of the Me.[24]

The material, social, and spiritual aspects of the Me can all be brought under the heading of "self-appreciation."

The I for James was "that which at any given moment *is* conscious, whereas the Me is only one of the things which it is conscious *of*."[25] There is an intellectual quality in the I which provides the terms whereby the self becomes a person through those self-regarding activities such as self-criticism, self-appraisal, etc. It is the Me that behaves and the I which

[21]*Ibid.*, p. 130.

[22]*Ibid.*, p. 191.

[23]W. H. Auden, "Hic et Ille," in *The Dyer's Hand* (New York: Random House, 1962), p. 93.

[24]William James, *Psychology* (Cleveland: The World Publishing Co., 1948), p. 181.

[25]*Ibid.*, p. 195.

understands the behavior. It is difficult to apprehend the I apart from the object of its interest, but James concludes that "the thoughts are the thinkers."[26]

James's conclusion about the nature of the I is provisional, but it does recommend a technique for representing the I in Chamber Theatre. When a literary character introspects, it may be appropriate to represent these thoughts, or state of mind, by a "thinker," a physical being, and to represent the object of the introspection by another physical being who stands in the position of the Me—material, social, and spiritual. Chamber Theatre actualizes a condition which is implicit in almost any discussion of the self: the poetic condition of personification. When Herbert J. Muller writes that "the self is not significant until it becomes aware of itself, capable of . . . 'the reflexive mood' in which it becomes both subject and object of an experience,"[27] we recognize the tendency to personify in order to establish discrete entities which are capable of some kind of sociophysical interactive awareness. It is impossible to talk about the self without using analogies. Chamber Theatre takes advantage of the poetic tendency to speak of the self in figurative language by extending the verbal image into the concrete world of the actual.

It is really not difficult to accept the self as *one* (subject-object) and then to view the same self as *two* (subject *and* object). Consider the phrase, "I smell," in its *transitive* condition which says, "I inhale an odor"; the subjective olfactory response is distinguished clearly from the objective nature of the odor. But when we consider the phrase, "I smell," in its *intransitive* condition which says, "I stink," the odor now has a subjective origin while the olfactory response is objectively located. When, in the *reflexive* mood "I smell" means that the odor I inhale is the same odor I, myself, exude—in other words, "I smell myself"—then Muller's description of self-awareness seems less analogical and more actual; the self as subject and object of an experience seems real enough. And so the I learns about the Me.

It is not so very different from learning about others, for we do so, according to George H. Mead, by assuming their attitudes, by momentarily taking up their role. Apparently it is the Me, the "socialized aspect of the personality" that puts itself in the place of others and the I becomes the self's *response* to the organized set of attitudes of others which the Me represents. The psychological technique for understanding others is, in these terms, not very different from that employed to gain self-understanding.

It is possible to have an aesthetic enjoyment of one's own experiences if one is able to put them in a disinterested perspective and regard

[26]*Ibid.*, p. 216.

[27] Herbert J. Muller, *Science and Criticism* (New York: George Braziller, 1956), p. 233.

them as happening to strangers. What is noteworthy is the similarity between the processes of self-awareness through the reflexive subject-object perspective and social intelligence through the object-subject perspective. Paul Schilder reminds us that it is the body-images of "others" that stimulate the formation of like attitudes within the observer, and it is to these imitations of others' attitudes that the observer responds. But for "strangers," the observer would have no self-knowledge.[28]

To be conscious of the I as distinct from the Me, to realize the extent to which the anima and the persona resist confrontation, to discriminate between subject and object, the knower and the known, requires constant practice. Through literature and the experimental situations it provides, it is possible to acquire new insights into the human condition, though the effort is much like pulling oneself up by one's own bootstraps. Nevertheless, it is possible in the field of fiction to observe the selves as interactive characters relating to each other spontaneously and serving as objectifications of our own inner life, promoting and projecting our own fantasies and unfulfilled wishes. It is always difficult in psychological matters to approach ourselves directly. We are fortunate then to be able to approach ourselves indirectly through our social intelligence, through our aesthetic depersonalization of our own experiences, and finally, tangentially, through the offices of art generally and literature specifically.

In the early phases of consciousness there is no selfhood for there is no awareness of the limits of the self, no clear boundary between inner and outer. There is no dividing line between perception and representation. The image does not stand for the object but is the object itself. What is perceived is real, since the person as yet, has no critical faculty with which to distinguish between reality and illusion. This early phase of consciousness is functional in Chamber Theatre where the self is divided and the separated elements are assigned to actors who, of course, appear in the flesh as complete entities. Although each performer clearly stands apart as a human being, there is a sense in which the self he or she represents is only one function of the total character. There is bifurcation, discreteness, and distinction, but there is no fatal or thoroughly artificial separation of the psychic elements. The antinomies are found in the division of the self into selves, on the one hand, and the absorption of each self into the total character (actor) as though it were his whole being. There is no tragic isolation of the self nor of the object: the object-self-character-actor is capable of metamorphosis, hovering between the subjective and the objective, between the illusion and the reality, between the dream and the outside world.

Experience, real or fictional, often involves a colloquy of selves,

---

[28]Schilder, *The Image and Appearance of the Human Body*, pp. 265-266.

asserting themselves, adjusting themselves to the needs and circumstances of the superself, real or imagined. Virginia Woolf speaks of this dialogue of selves in her essay, "Evening Over Essex: Reflections in a Motor Car." Miss Woolf was impressed with the beauty of Essex in the evening twilight but she could not understand why there was a "sediment of irritation" in her. She felt that the explanation lay in the area of her soul that resented the impotency she felt at not being able to hold the moment of beauty, to overcome it, to master it. She says in the essay:

> But relinquish, I said (it is well known how in circumstances like these the self splits up and one self is eager and dissatisfied and the other stern and philosophical), relinquish these impossible aspirations; be content with the view in front of us, and believe me when I tell you it is best to sit and soak . . .
>
> While these two selves then held a colloquy about the wise course to adopt in the presence of beauty, I (a third party now declared itself) said to myself, how happy they were to enjoy so simple an occupation. There they sat as the car sped along, noticing everything: a hay stack; a rust red roof; a pond . . . But I, being somewhat different, sat aloof and melancholy. While they are thus busied, I said to myself: Gone, gone; over, over; past and done with, past and done with. I feel life left behind even as the road is left behind. . . .
>
> Then suddenly a fourth self (a self which lies in ambush apparently dormant, and jumps upon one unawares. Its remarks are often entirely disconnected with what has been happening, but must be attended to because of their abruptness) said: "Look at that." It was a light; brilliant, freakish; inexplicable. For a second I was unable to name it. "A star"; and for that second . . . it danced and beamed. "I take your meaning," I said. "You, erratic and impulsive self that you are, feel that the light over the downs there emerging, dangles from the future. . . ."[29]

Virginia Woolf has plainly marked off for us four possible selves that might engage in an experience and she has been explicit about what it is they say in their colloquies as well as being specific about their actions. She recognizes, too, that there is a host, a single personality, within whom these selves have their corporate being. Miss Woolf's essay demonstrates very effectively the character of the self with its refracted elements and recommends speech and action for those elements in as much detail as one could ask of any promptscript for a Chamber Theatre production.

---

[29]From "Evening Over Sussex" in *The Death of the Moth* by Virginia Woolf, copyright © 1942 by Harcourt Brace Jovanovich, Inc.; copyright © 1970 by Marjorie T. Parsons, Executrix. Reprinted by permission of the publishers and the Hogarth Press.

3

POINT OF VIEW

FIRST-PERSON NARRATOR: MAJOR CHARACTER

Traditionally, the first-person narrator is a storyteller who narrates events using the ego pronoun "I," when referring to him or herself. This person generally addresses the reader directly while, at the same time, carrying on a fictive life with other characters in the story. In other words, this narrator relates personally both to characters "inside" the story and to the reader "outside" the story.

As a storyteller "outside" the story the first-person narrator shares the same time and place with the reader or audience but as a character "inside" the story he or she relives experiences that have already happened at some time in the past. It is important to know the narrator's "epic situation," that is, the vantage point from which the story is told. Bertil Romberg suggests that

> . . . the epic situation . . . supplies the answer to important questions about epic time and why the novel is narrated, and also supplies effective support for that illusion of reality which it may be the purpose of the novel to evoke.[1]

---

[1]Bertil Romberg, *Studies in the Narrative Technique of the First-Person Novel* (Stockholm: Almkvist and Wiksell, 1962), p. 33. Reprinted with the permission of the author.

The duality of the first-person narrator's situation provides the complex dynamics of Chamber Theatre staging. The narrator and the audience relate to each other directly for they are together in time and place; the narrator as a character in the story relates to the other characters directly for they share a remembered time and place, while the audience and the characters in the story relate to each other indirectly for they have their existence in different times and places. More succintly, we can say that the audience is in one time and place, the characters in another time and place, while the narrator-character alternates his existence between both settings.

The epic situation for the first-person narrator often has a built-in duality: "he both narrates and experiences, he is both old and young; it is certainly a case of identical persons, and yet they are not the same person."[2] Sometimes an author will separate the elements in the duality by using the ego pronoun for one aspect of the narrator and the third person (proper noun or personal pronoun) for the other. The separation of the experiencing narrator from the narrating storyteller, whether it is in time or in space, or both, is at the root of the problem of duality. A solution offered by Chamber Theatre is the use of two actors to represent the two separate elements into which the narrator has been divided.

In Günter Grass's novel, *The Tin Drum*, the spatial aspect of the epic situation is established with the narrator's opening statement: "I am an inmate of a mental hospital."[3] The epic situation is further clarified when the narrator says, "My keeper . . . has bought me five hundred sheets of writing paper,"[4] and, "I found my fountain pen in the drawer beside the photograph album: it's full, ink is no problem, how shall I begin?"[5] After some discussion of the various ways to begin a story, the narrator says, "And so to you personally, dear reader . . . I introduce Oskar's maternal grandmother. Late one October afternoon my grandmother . . ."[6] So "Oskar's" grandmother is "my" grandmother and therefore Oskar and I are one character. Dualism has set in: there is an oral narrator and one who is writing; there is a little boy and an inmate in a hospital; there is "Oskar" and there is "I." The epic situation is divided spatially and temporally. A Chamber Theatre staging of Grass's novel would very likely use two actors in the epic situation in order to demonstrate that the narrator is bifurcated.

The photograph album is a significant source of memory for the

---

[2]*Ibid.*, p. 36.

[3]Günter Grass, *The Tin Drum* trans. Ralph Manheim (New York: Pantheon Books, 1961), p. 15. Reprinted by permission of Random House, Inc.

[4]*Ibid.*, p. 16.

[5]*Ibid.*, p. 17.

[6]*Ibid.*, p. 18.

narrator's fictitious memoir. He says, "What novel . . . can have the epic scope of a photograph album?"[7] The bifurcated narrator is self-related in terms of the album: "I am guarding a treasure . . . during the trip in the freight car I clutched it to my breast, and when I slept, Oskar slept on his treasure, his photograph album."[8]

Consider Vladimir Nabokov's novel, *Lolita*, whose first-person narrator, Humbert Humbert, seems on first acquaintance to be speaking from an epic situation which is oral.[9] On the first page of the novel, Humbert Humbert addresses the "ladies and gentlemen of the jury" and proceeds to tell them of his early life: "I was born in 1910, in Paris."[10] However, the family history is not entirely a matter of oral recollection. Humbert Humbert passes around to the jury some picture postcards. The oralized evidence is supported by pictorial evidence; on the fifth page of the novel the narrator says, "I leaf again and again through these miserable memories . . ."[11] giving the reader a sense of the picture album and of recollections at the same time. On the eleventh page Humbert Humbert says, "Let me remind my reader . . ."[12] and soon we learn that what started out as an oral address to the jury has become a written manuscript composed in his prison cell. The act of composition provides Humbert Humbert with the kind of objectivity he needs for self-understanding and it leads to his written references to himself in the third person: "Humbert Humbert tried hard to be good."[13] A few pages later he starts the practice of addressing himself: "I told myself . . ."[14] This reflexive construction becomes rather common in the novel and leads to an appreciation of what we are told in the fictitious Foreword —that Humbert Humbert, the "author's bizarre cognomen is his own invention; and, of course, this mask—through which two hypnotic eyes seem to glow—had to remain unlifted in accordance with its wearer's wishes."[15]

The complexities of the point of view of the first-person narrator in *Lolita* would require a Chamber Theatre presentation employing at least two actors for the character of Humbert Humbert—one in the prison at work on his manuscript and one who is referred to in the third person and who is active in the recollected life of the hero.

[7]*Ibid.*, p. 49.

[8]*Ibid.*, p. 49.

[9]Vladimir Nabokov, *Lolita* (New York: G. P. Putnam's Sons, 1955). Reprinted with the permission of the publisher.

[10]*Ibid.*, p. 11.

[11]*Ibid.*, p. 15.

[12]*Ibid.*, p. 21.

[13]*Ibid.*, p. 21.

[14]*Ibid.*, p. 27.

[15]*Ibid.*, p. 5.

John Barth's *End of the Road* is told by a first-person narrator who opens the novel with the identification of his own refracted character—"In a sense, I am Jacob Horner."[16] It is not uncommon for first-person narrators to identify themselves by name, as in *Moby-Dick*, when the teller of the tale announces himself—"Call me Ishmael." But in Barth's novel there is an element of refraction created by the phrase, "in a sense," which suggests that the relationship between the proper name, "Jacob Horner," and the ego pronoun "I" is not clear and may even be arguable. In any case we are not surprised to learn that Horner is undergoing psychiatric treatment.

The slight dissociation created by the phrase, "in a sense," takes a rather more severe form in Chapter Four of *End of the Road:*

> . . . all the way home it was as though there were no Jacob Horner today. . . . On these days Jacob Horner, except in a meaningless metabolistic sense, ceased to exist altogether, for I was without a personality . . .[17]

We learn half way through the novel that Horner is capable of maintaining "with perfectly equal unenthusiasm contradictory, or at least polarized, opinions at once on a given subject." It seemed to Jacob Horner "that Jacob Horner—owl, peacock, chameleon, donkey, and popinjay, fugitive from a medieval bestiary—was at the same time giant and dwarf, plenum and vacuum, and admirable and contemptible."[18] Skillful assignment of lines to be spoken by two actors would make clear to an audience the polarities of Horner's character and dramatize the stasis or inanition created by the unresolved tension of his conflicts. As in *Lolita* there would seem to be some advantage in staging Barth's novel with two actors in the role of Jacob Horner.

The first chapter of J. P. Donleavy's novel, *The Ginger Man*,[19] begins with six lines of narration in the third person and is followed by two pages of dialogue involving two characters, O'Keefe and Sebastian Dangerfield, uninterrupted by any narration whatsoever. This proportion of narration and dialogue persists until the middle of the second chapter when the third-person narration slips with no transition into first-person narration. Until this point in the story, O'Keefe and Dangerfield have been referred to in the third person in the narration, but now there is a shift:

[16]John Barth, *End of the Road* (rev. ed.; New York: Doubleday & Co., 1967), p. 1. Reprinted with the permission of the publisher.

[17]*Ibid.*, pp. 32-33.

[18]*Ibid.*, p. 114.

[19]J. P. Donleavy, *The Ginger Man* (New York: Berkeley Medallion Books, 1965). Reprinted by permission of the publisher.

The toasted bird was put on the green table. O'Keefe driving a fork into the dripping breast and ripping off the legs. Pot gives a tremble on the shelf. Little curtains with red spots flutter. A gale outside. When you think of it O'Keefe can cook. And this is my first chicken since the night I left New York and the waiter asked me if I wanted to keep the menu as a memory and I sat there in the blue carpeted room and said yes.[20]

Since the narrator has been referring to Dangerfield in the third person and Dangerfield himself has only spoken in direct discourse with quotation marks setting off his speeches, the reader is not prepared for his speaking in the first person—"This is my first chicken"—without quotation marks. He is not speaking to O'Keefe, but to himself, perhaps, for the passage is a memory. As if to make sure that the reader understands this passage to be an interior monologue, the direct discourse within the memory—"and said yes"—is printed without quotation marks enclosing the word "yes."

This pattern is followed throughout the novel. The narration, which concerns the present circumstances and interactions of the characters existing in the present moment, is expressed in the third person, whereas the narration that expresses the inner thoughts and feelings as well as the recollections or fantasy projections of Sebastian Dangerfield is spoken in the first person. Again, it would seem necessary to have two actors in the role of Dangerfield in order to dramatize the shifts in person.

An interesting development in the point of view occurs on the final pages of the novel. Sebastian is alone and engaged in one of his internal monologues, spoken, as usual, in the first person and involving dialogue with others, but without benefit of quotation marks. The passage begins with a first-person reference—"I must stop and look through these busted grimy windows"—and then continues with a shift to the third person in referring to himself—"He was walking down the slope side of the bridge past this broken building, a straight dark figure and stranger." Then there is a shift back to the first person with a second person involved—is it the other Dangerfield, the reader, or the Ginger Man? The narrator says, "Come here till I tell you." No quotation marks appear in the original. Grant the ambiguity of the pronominal referent "you" and say that we are all caught up, Sebastian, the narrator, the reader, all of us in the final lines of the novel:

> God's mercy
> On the wild
> Ginger Man.[21]

[20]*Ibid.*, p. 16.
[21]*Ibid.*, p. 304.

A Chamber Theatre production of *The Ginger Man* might do well to feature two actors in the role of Sebastian Dangerfield with the intention of dramatizing for the audience the bifurcation of his character, the unredeemed and the unredeemable, the natural and the unnatural man. One actor would speak the external dialogue, the other would speak the internal monologue. A third actor should then be used to speak the objective narration. The picture we now have of the novel is that there is a Dangerfield who lives an internal life with its memories and fantasies while a second Dangerfield lives an external life with O'Keefe, Mary, Miss Frost, etc., and still another Dangerfield who tells his own story in the third person with an artist's objectivity and control.

FIRST-PERSON NARRATOR:
MINOR CHARACTER

An author can minimize the disadvantage of the limited and prejudicial view of a first-person narrator by creating a *minor character* who comments on the events of the main story from a peripheral or dispassionate position. This minor character is still "inside" the story and speaks in the first person, thereby preserving the authenticity of an eyewitness account; but a minor character's emotional involvement and responsibilities to the plot are marginal rather than central. His or her view of the action of the story can be somewhat more reliable. The major character who reports in the first person will render a subjective point of view from inside the story, whereas the minor character, also reporting in the first person from inside the story, will render a somewhat more objective point of view. Nevertheless, minor characters who narrate stories may exercise a subtle and persuasive control over the reader's sensibilities.

The epic situation for "Fred," the first-person narrator of Truman Capote's novel, *Breakfast at Tiffany's*,[22] is that of the written memoir. "Fred" is a young writer who might be expected to look out on the world as source material for his art. Capote moderates this view of the calculating author by suggesting that "Fred's" motivation for recording his recollections of Holly Golightly, the principal character in the novel, is spontaneously prompted by a revisit to the old neighborhood where he first met the heroine:

> It never occurred to me in those days to write about Holly Golightly, and probably it would not now except for a conversation I had with Joe Bell that set the whole memory of her in motion again.[23]

[22]Truman Capote, *Breakfast at Tiffany's* (New York: Random House, 1958).
[23]*Ibid.*, p. 3.

"Fred" met Holly under the accidental circumstances of living in the same apartment house with the young girl. He is in much the same condition as the reader; he sees and hears only what we see and hear. No preconceptions are involved, no blood kinship, no formal introduction provides any special circumstances. Yet "Fred" is "in touch" with Holly and since the reader is "in touch" with "Fred" and he with the reader there is a sense in which the reader is "in touch" with Holly.

As "Fred" is drawn more and more deeply into the entangled skein of Holly's existence and his emotional attachment to her deepens, we find ourselves, the readers, following in the wake of the narrator. The narrator, like the reader, begins his adventure in the novel as an outsider, an observer, but as he is drawn into the action his responses become more subjective as do those of the reader. We conclude that the epic situation of the narrator is so conceived by the author that the reader is led rather than forced into a sympathetic understanding of a character whose personality might ordinarily be expected to alienate the reader's affections.

In F. Scott Fitzgerald's *The Great Gatsby*,[24] the first-person narrator, Nick Carraway, seems, in the early passages of the novel, to be the major character, but with the introduction of Gatsby himself, the reader reconsiders and thereafter relegates Nick to the role of minor character. He came East from a Middle Western city to seek his fortune as a young man in New York. His associations, direct and indirect, with Gatsby constitute the bulk of the novel. But with the death of Gatsby there still remains one-tenth of the story to be told. If the novel had for its exclusive interest the adventures of Gatsby, its title figure, Fitzgerald would have run a risk of creating an anticlimax by letting the story run on for another thirteen pages. What he accomplishes, in those last pages, however, is the restoration of the narrator to his central position in the novel. As a result of his experiences with Gatsby, who "believed in the green light, the orgiastic future that year by year recedes before us,"[25] Nick learns that the dream is elusive because it is behind us "where the dark fields of the republic rolled on under the night." The narrator is the only character in the novel who has been changed in any significant way by his association with Gatsby. The change is manifest by the reversal of Nick's directions. At the beginning of the story we find him seeking his fortune in the East, but after the death of Gatsby he seeks the realization of his dream, which in some respects is Gatsby's dream too, in the West, or more precisely the Middle West, Nick's original home.

What Chamber Theatre can do in the staging of stories told by

[24]F. Scott Fitzgerald, *The Great Gatsby*, reprinted in *The Portable F. Scott Fitzgerald* (New York: Viking Press, 1945).

[25]*Ibid.*, p. 168.

first-person narrators who are minor characters is to place them physically where they can be observant, but not central. They need not be shunted to the side to take up their position forlornly by the proscenium arch and to make as little movement as possible. It should be obvious that no first-person narrator is ever that inconspicuous. Generally speaking, the first-person narrator who is a minor character echoes or reflects the point of view the author wishes his/her readers or audience to take. The best position for the narrator then would be somewhere between the audience and the action, a position that stresses a mediating role between the audience and the action of the principal characters. This would not be a fixed position, of course, because such narrators would at times be called on to participate in the action as do "Fred" and Nick in the novels we have discussed. They are authentic "I" witnesses, but they are participants, too, and the shifting relationships must be reflected in the physical movement of the narrators in and out of the action according to the extent of their subjective or objective commitment.

THIRD-PERSON NARRATOR: OMNISCIENT

Some authors, impatient of the limitations of the angle of vision imposed on the first-person narrator, require a storyteller who is capable of exploring the motivations and inner recesses of the characters in the story. Or, at the very least, they would like to present the inner life of a particular character to a reader in such fashion as would make the report altogether reliable. Such a narrator would be privy to the dreams, private thoughts, and feelings of the characters and also be able to report simultaneous actions from a number of different places: in a word, he/she would be omniscient. This impartial narrator speaks in the third person from outside the story and, as such, is not physically characterized by the author nor recognized by the characters in the story.

The omniscient narrator is especially useful when the author is dealing with a character who is unaware of the motives at work in him or herself, or who lacks sufficient command of language to express them. In William Faulkner's "Barn Burning"[26] the narrator enjoys limited omniscience with respect to the "poor white" boy with the prepossessing name, Colonel Sartoris Snopes. On some occasions the omniscient narrator reports the boy's inner thoughts in the corrupt language which is native to the boy: "*He aims for me to lie*, he thought," or "*Hit's big as a courthouse*, he thought quietly." Notice that the colloquial diction creates

[26]William Faulkner, "Barn Burning," in *Short Story Masterpieces*, eds. Robert Penn Warren and Albert Erskine (New York: Dell Publishing Co., 1954). Reprinted by permission of Random House, Inc.

the illusion that we are hearing the boy's thoughts directly without any mediation by a narrator; notice, too, the use of italics to set off the boy's inner speech from the narrator's speech, a stylistic device established by Faulkner early in the story.

On other occasions, however, the boy's inner thoughts are beyond his expressive capacities and the narrator takes over for him. The narrator tells the reader he is taking over for the boy when he says, "the surge of peace and joy whose reasons he [the boy] could not have thought into words, being too young for that"[27] and proceeds immediately in italics to say:

> *They are safe from him* [the boy's father]. *People whose lives are a part of this peace and dignity are beyond his touch . . . the spell of this peace and dignity rendering even the barns and stable and cribs which belong to it impervious to the puny flames he might contrive.*[28]

The use of italics indicate that these thoughts, though not the words, are indeed those of the boy.

A Chamber Theatre presentation of the relationship between the narrator and the boy in "Barn Burning" might well regard the narrator as a projection of the boy into maturity, or more simply as an educated voice giving expression to the boy's inchoate thoughts and feelings. In staging the relationship we would expect to find the narrator physically close to the boy when he is sharing or expressing the latter's inner life. The narrator would be close to the boy whenever he is making objective observations seen from the boy's angle of vision, for example, "Presently he [the boy] could see the grove of oaks. . . ."[29] Whenever the vision of the narrator includes some objective reference to the boy himself, he would have to maintain a certain distance from the boy, for example, "The boy was chopping wood behind the house. . . ."[30] The narrator's physical relation to the boy takes on a dynamic quality when the text shifts quickly from the objective observations to the subjective responses. At the opening of the story the narrator says, "The boy, crouched on his nail keg at the back of the crowded room, knew he smelled cheese."[31] The narrator is at some remove from the boy during the objective references to the nail keg and the room, but he is moving toward the boy so that he can be close to him for the omniscient reference to the smelling of the cheese which is a subjective state. Shifting from the objective to the subjective points of view provides the dynamics of the narrator's actions

27*Ibid.*, p. 168.
28*Ibid.*, p. 168.
29*Ibid.*, p. 168.
30*Ibid.*, p. 170.
31*Ibid.*, p. 162.

in the story. Though he is categorized as omniscient, he cannot be seen as peripheral or static in his behavior.

An author will sometimes let the narrator qualify his omniscience with an expression of supposition, thereby avoiding the direct and positive naming of a state of mind or heart. Melville, in "Benito Cereno,"[32] found it necessary, because of the nature of the story, to reveal rather fully the thoughts and feelings of Captain Delano. He allowed his omniscient narrator a certain indirectness, however, through the use of such words as "perhaps," when identifying an interior state:

> Perhaps it was some such influence as above is attempted to be described which, in Captain Delano's mind, heightened whatever, upon a staid scrutiny, . . . might have seemed unusual.[33]

The narrator's modesty here is evident in his suggestion that "perhaps" he has identified what it is that heightened the Captain's sense of the unusual.

In *Washington Square*, Henry James permitted the narrator to use the same device for mitigating omniscience: "It was *perhaps* [italics supplied], however, because Mrs. Penniman suspected them that she said no more that evening about Morris Townsend."[34] Here again, the word "perhaps" softens the nonhuman quality that generally characterizes the omniscient narrator.

Sometimes the function of the omniscient narrator is simply to gain entry to the inner life of the character and to make the reader relatively comfortable in this position of intimacy. In James Joyce's short story, "The Boarding House,"[35] the omniscient narrator observed Mrs. Mooney rather closely as she

> . . . glanced instinctively at the little gilt clock on the mantelpiece. . . . It was seventeen minutes past eleven: she would have lots of time to have the matter out with Mr. Doran and then catch short twelve at Marlborough Street."[36]

The narrator's observation of Mrs. Mooney's glance at the clock is only tinged with omniscience when he interprets her objective action as instinctive. His omniscience increases, however, when he presumes to

[32]Herman Melville, "Benito Cereno," in *The House of Fiction*, eds. Caroline Gordon and Allen Tate (New York: Charles Scribner's Sons, 1950).

[33]*Ibid.*, p. 43.

[34]Henry James, *Washington Square*, reprinted in *Great American Short Novels*, ed. William Phillips (New York: Dial Press, 1946). Reprinted with the permission of Alexander R. James.

[35]James Joyce, "The Boarding House," in *Short Story Masterpieces*, eds. Robert Penn Warren and Albert Erskine (New York: Dell Publishing Co., 1954). Reprinted by permission of The Viking Press, Inc.

[36]*Ibid.*, p. 234.

know that she is thinking that she will have time for her talk with Mr. Doran before the last mass served at the church in Marlborough Street. Notice, however, that we are not entirely dependent on the narrator's superior powers of penetration; the impression is subtly conveyed to the reader that he is hearing the very words of Mrs. Mooney's thoughts without the intercession of the narrator. Joyce creates this effect by shifting the diction from the customary formality of the remainder of the narration to the colloquial diction of Mrs. Mooney's social class. When the narrator says "have the matter out" and "catch short twelve" he is using Mrs. Mooney's language, not his own, and we are under the momentary illusion that we are hearing the landlady's direct expression of her thoughts. Such a device eases the unnatural strain of unqualified omniscience.

In a Chamber Theatre presentation of this section of Joyce's tale the narrator would tell the audience that "Mrs. Mooney glanced instinctively at the little gilt clock on the mantelpiece" and would himself examine the clock a little more closely to assure himself of the exact time before he said, "It was seventeen minutes past eleven." In Joyce's text a colon follows the word "eleven"; it is a common punctuation device used throughout the story in a rather special way which creates the general effect of dialogue, the narrator on one side of the colon and the character on the other. The distribution of the narration, then, would be as follows:

NAR: It was seventeen minutes past eleven:

MRS. M: She would have lots of time to have the matter out with Mr. Doran and then catch short twelve at Marlborough Street.

There is an ambivalence created by this distribution that gives a certain imaginative flavor to Chamber Theatre. The narrator tells us the time by the clock, but it is Mrs. Mooney who glanced at the clock and it is her reading of the time that we are hearing. In other words, the narrator is both his own omniscient self *and* Mrs. Mooney. When Mrs. Mooney refers to herself in the third person with the pronoun "she" we accept the awkwardness for she is being not only herself but also her own narrator. Put briefly, the narrator is in part the character and the character is in part the narrator. A fuller discussion of the aesthetics of characters referring to themselves in the third person in narrative passages will be developed later.

THIRD-PERSON NARRATOR: OBJECTIVE OBSERVER

The epic situation of the objective observer is outside the story. Such a narrator must remain entirely objective and reliable so that the readership, left to its own interpretative devices, may nevertheless trust the evidence that the narrator presents. The objective observer, like most of us, must be content to report only what he or she sees and hears as a human being living at a particular time and in a specific place. Unlike most of us, however, the objective storyteller may not pass on to the reader any peculiar biased views of the events. Stories narrated by objective observers are closely related to the drama; they provide the reader with identifications of time and place and give stage directions which describe the appearance and actions of the characters. Interpretation is scrupulously avoided. What is here described is a seldom-realized ideal, a hermetic objectivity.

That objective narrators rarely succeed in being thoroughly objective will surprise no one, for it must be repeated that an act of pure perception, however desirable, is not possible. Human beings by nature observe selectively and this in itself is a form of interpretation. All spoken observations entail certain tones of voice and attitudes that lend them an aura of subjectivity. Literature reflects the same tendency. In A. E. Coppard's story, "The Third Prize,"[37] the objective observer begins on the very first page to show signs of subjectivity. Two young clerks, very likely from London, arrive at a midland town in England to find

> . . . almost the entire populace wending to the carnival of games in a long stream of soldiers, sailors, and quite ordinary people, harried by pertinacious and vociferous little boys . . .[38]

The narrator in this passage reveals by his diction a certain comic superiority. One may, in a fit of formality, refer to the people of a small midland town as "populace," but it is indeed unusual to slip into an archaic expression like "wending" to indicate their going to the Fair, which this narrator calls "carnival of games." Further subjectivity is hinted at in the use of words like "pertinacious" and "vociferous," adjectives distinctly out of key with the commonplace characters of the story. The whole elevated tone of the formal diction and romantic images which suggest the dignity of the Greek Olympic games creates an atmosphere of comic contrast to the Midland Fair.

It may seem advisable in the staging of objective narration to keep the narrator at a discrete distance from the action so that objectivity is not jeopardized. However, objectivity does not always depend on physical removal from the observed event. The umpire and the referee are most reliable when they are close to the event. The surgeon is objective

[37]A. E. Coppard, "The Third Prize," in *Short Story Masterpieces,* eds. Robert Penn Warren and Albert Erskine (New York: Dell Publishing Co., 1954).

[38]*Ibid.,* p. 115.

during the course of an operation, but inevitably intimate in relating to the patient. The objective observer, when narrating a description of a character's moist palms, foul breath, or dirty fingernails, had better not be too far away from that character. That is to say, the narrator must maintain that distance from the object or action which is appropriate to the nature of the observation.

The art of prose fiction has its formal laws despite an infinite variety of exceptions. Point of view, as a means of controlling the operation of the central intelligence responsible for the telling of a story, has certain categorical limitations demanding a modicum of consistency. But if the "house of fiction" has innumerable windows representing modified points of view, then categorical distinctions seem unprofitable. The same may be said of the fundamental distinctions between showing and telling a story. Booth rightly insists that "the line between showing and telling is always to some degree an arbitrary one."[39] Narration as an art must submit to law, aesthetic law; it must show a systematic development in the course of a work. Yet the critic must be reluctant to count heavily on consistency. Close examination of a single work, as we have seen, will inevitably undermine the critic's temptation to overgeneralize.

It is the central concern of Chamber Theatre to present on the stage the dynamic relationship between the lyric (that is, the element wherein the audience is addressed in the telling of the story) and the dramatic elements of narrative literature. The narrator, the lyric element in fiction, controls the aesthetic image, while the characters constitute the dramatic element, behaving with apparent free will and responding to each other with seeming spontaneity. The dramatic element is traditionally at home on the stage, but the lyric element is generally suppressed in a theatrical presentation. Whenever a narrator's services are required in a play, he or she is frequently found on the periphery of the main action, only occasionally entering to describe a change of scene or to summarize events.

Chamber Theatre insists on altering the convention that bars narration from the stage; it restores to the narrator his/her powers of directing and, indeed, creating the story. It is well to begin with the notion that the narrator is stage center, for that is the position of strongest control, and from which the characters may be called upon to lend the story vigor and immediacy. When a narrator chooses to feature certain characters by letting them speak in their own person and perform their own action, then he/she retires to a less central position. In the omniscient condition, the narrator must assume a position physically close to the character, but as an objective observer he/she may be at some distance from the main

---

[39]Wayne C. Booth, *The Rhetoric of Fiction* (Chicago, Ill.: University of Chicago Press, 1961), p. 20. Reprinted with the permission of the publishers.

action, affording the audience perhaps a panoramic view or "long shot." Such a stance may just as plausibly, however, reveal the minuscule features of a character's face, as the narrator moves in for a "close-up."

First-person narrators will behave in accordance with the general laws of dramatic action on the stage when they are actively relating to other characters in the story. When they are narrating out of sight and sound of the other characters then they will relate to the audience by drawing closer to it.

Wayne Booth's warning that distinctions of person may be overworked should serve us in this discussion of the various behaviors of narrators on stage. We will follow Booth's further suggestion that we only learn something of importance about narration when we "describe how the particular qualities of the narrator relate to specific effects." In other words, the true value of a Chamber Theatre presentation of any point of view is seen in the application of staging techniques to specific stories.

4

STYLE

Just as Chamber Theatre makes a story's point of view physically evident in the behavior of the narrator so does it physically realize the style of the story. The narration appears on the printed page as a written style which becomes, in the transfer to the stage, a spoken style with the addition of intonational patterns, pauses, vocal emphasis, and other paralinguistic elements. As the narrator moves about the stage his/her nonverbal behavior is expected to be consonant with the style in which he/she speaks. In literature, as in life, there is a measure of consistency in the personalities of individuals which leads us to expect that one's verbal and nonverbal behavior will be congruent. The metaphors used by critics to describe a specific narrative style should apply with equal justice to the behavior of the particular narrator employing that style. If the style of the narration can be said to be stiff, awkward, or pedestrian, we can expect the narrator to behave in the same fashion; if the style of the narration, on the other hand, is smooth, elegant, and graceful, we will not be surprised to find the narrator's nonverbal manner much the same.

It is probably not possible to settle on any definition of style that will serve all literary discussions. Style has often been regarded as ornamentation, or it has been thought of as the *manner* in which the *matter* of a text is conveyed, and the manner must always be at the service of the matter. A more contemporary view of style in literature continues to see it as manner but relegates the matter to simply a *context* in which we experience the true value of the literature—this being its style or form.

If we augment the definition of style as "a thinking out into language" to include feeling as a condition of human experience that can be externalized in language, we have a definition sufficiently large to accommodate our discussion. But we need to agree further that written language is a dialect of spoken language and that gesture is as much a feature of spoken language as it is of nonverbal communication. The most succinct way of putting it is to say that language is action. It is the function of Chamber Theatre to express the style of the written dialect in spoken form and to augment the spoken style with consonant or congruent gestural behavior.

Alfred North Whitehead has good advice for the interpreter of literary style. He suggests that "the sense of style . . . is an aesthetic sense, based on admiration for the direct attainment of a foreseen end, simply and without waste."[1] The interpreter who recognizes that style is a working rule and not an arbitrary or accidental concomitant, that it is efficiently designed for a specific effect, will seek to implement it accordingly. The necessity for voicing and performing the style of a specific Chamber Theatre production will compel the interpreter to move consistently toward the "foreseen end." To accomplish the end "simply and without waste" does not mean that a baroque style, for example, is to be stripped of its convolutions in the interest of simplification, or that all elaborations or iterations are necessarily wasteful. Whitehead asks the appreciative reader to recognize just how effectively style achieves, qualitatively and quantitatively, the author's foreseen aesthetic end. Economy in style is to be gauged by the demands of the end: only as much elaboration as an elaborate end calls for, only as much polychromatic richness as is necessary to create a baroque effect should be used.

Often the narrator will adopt the diction or style of a character when expressing that character's inner thoughts or feelings. In Nelson Algren's story, "A Bottle of Milk for Mother," a young man is explaining to Captain Kozak of the Chicago police: "This has sure been one good lesson for me. Now I'll go to a big-ten collitch 'n make good you."[2] His speech reveals him as a Polish-American speaking in the dialect of that ethnic group. In the narration that follows this passage, spoken by an omniscient third person outside the story, we sense that Bicek, rather than the narrator, is responsible for the thoughts because of the language or style of the narration:

That ought to set Kozak back awhile, they might even send

---

[1]Alfred North Whitehead, *The Aims of Education and Other Essays* (New York: Mentor Books, 1949), p. 24. Reprinted by permission of Macmillan Publishing Co. and George Allen and Unwin Ltd.

[2]Nelson Algren, "A Bottle of Milk for Mother," in *Short Story Masterpieces* (New York: Dell Publishing Co., 1954), p. 39.

him to a bug doc. He'd have to be careful—not too screwy. Just screwy enough to get by without involving Benkowski.[3]

With the exception of the word "involving," the diction is that of Bicek and not that of the narrator.

Later in the story the narrator expresses his own observations of Bicek's behavior, observations that hint at omniscience but may only be sympathetic identification:

Bicek forced himself to grin good-naturedly. He was getting pretty good, these last couple of days, at grinning under pressure. When a fellow got sore he couldn't think straight, he reflected anxiously. And so he yawned in Kozak's face with deliberateness, stretching himself as effortlessly as a cat.[4]

The first two sentences of this quotation are semi-formal in consonance with the narrator's style but allowing for certain informalities, like "getting pretty good," to reflect the presence of Bicek. When the narrator speaks in his own right, providing the sign of indirect discourse, "he reflected anxiously," the style becomes formal and distinctly unlike that of Bicek.

When the diction of the omniscient narrator reflects the diction of the character with whom he or she is omniscient, the reader may be disposed to regard the narration as biased and thus to begin to delineate the narrator's character. It is the function of Chamber Theatre staging to make more explicit, perhaps, the process of definition and to vivify for the audience the qualities of the narrator that so often go unnoticed or unappreciated.

Any critical interest in literature includes an interest in the primary level of stylistic usage, the author's specific purpose, which is that of directing the reader's responses. One way of apprehending the author's intention is to examine the narration and pay close attention to the relationship between the style of the narration and the tone of the story. When the narration is spoken by a character within the story his or her personality may be apprehended through self-revelation, through the remarks of others, and, of course, through the character's own external behavior.

However, when the narration is spoken by someone outside the story, then the reader's clues are severely limited to matters of style, that is, the selection and arrangement of words. Sometimes, a sharp contrast between the style of the third-person narrator and that of the characters within the story can reveal the narrator's quality.

The point of view in O. Henry's short story, "The Furnished Room," is that of a third-person narrator telling the tale of an ordinary

[3]*Ibid.*, p. 39.
[4]*Ibid.*, p. 41.

young man who is wandering in the slums of New York City looking for his sweetheart who has presumably left her small town to seek her fortune in the big city. The story opens with this description of the denizens of the lower West Side:

> Restless, shifting, fugacious as time itself is a certain vast bulk of the population of the red brick district of the lower West Side. Homeless, they have a hundred homes. They flit from furnished room to furnished room, transients forever—transients in abode, transients in heart and mind. They sing, "Home, Sweet Home" in ragtime; they carry their *lares et penates* in a bandbox; their vine is entwined about a picture hat; a rubber plant is their fig tree.[5]

The narrator's use of latinated diction—"fugacious," "transients," "population"—suggests a tone somewhat depersonalized and remote; certainly "fugacious" is not in current use among slum dwellers and is, therefore, a little too grand for the occasion.

There is a slight literary posturing in the syntactical inversion in the first sentence—"Restless . . . is . . . the population." The second sentence is a paradox which draws the reader's attention to the narrator's wit rather than to the scene of the West Side. When the narrator speaks in the third sentence of "they," flitting from room to room, the reader gets an impression of movement more appropriate to Tinker Bell than to the hapless indigents whom we would generally think of as listless, depressed, and heavy-footed. In the same sentence the storyteller employs alliteration, repetition of words and phrases until the brief sentence achieves an emotional intensity distinctly lyrical. The series of contrasted images that makes up the final sentence in the first paragraph approaches stylistic indulgence. The reader becomes increasingly aware of the narrator's inventions, but less sure of their relevance to the subject.

The latinated diction, the poetic inversions, the lyrical repetitions, and the strained contrasts suggest the self-conscious narrator who is showing off a little and, because his display is inappropriate to his subject, the final effect is one of pretension. These effects are not peculiar to the opening paragraph but are characteristic of the narration throughout the story. The previous occupants of the furnished room are outlandishly referred to as "divers tenantry," while the floor-covering is described in terms that suggest a young journalist with literary pretensions posturing before his muse: "A polychromatic rug like some brilliant-flowered rectangular islet lay surrounded by a billowy sea of soiled matting."[6]

A Chamber Theatre production of O. Henry's story would ask of its

---

[5]O. Henry, "The Furnished Room," in *The Four Million* (New York: Doubleday, 1912), p. 239. Reprinted with the permission of the publisher.
[6]*Ibid.*, p. 243.

narrator that he speak with arched superiority, affected diction, and a lyrical tone of voice. He would posture and pose, listen more to the sound of his own words than look out at the scene around him. He might wear white gloves, evening clothes, and carry a cane. His costume would be out of character for the setting and that fact would serve as an analogue of his verbal style which is also out of character for the setting. He would not touch anything, nor let anything touch him; when he refers to the "polychromatic rug" he might lift the dirty rag with the tip of his cane. He could also use his cane to point airily at a "trifling vase or two" in the room. There would be something of the stock actor's mannerisms in the narrator's behavior, matching the artificial, poetic affectations and stilted diction of O. Henry's text.

When dealing with a third-person narrator who remains outside the action of the story, it is tempting to regard him/her in the light of a Chinese prop man, who, by convention, is invisible and merely tolerated as a mechanical necessity. The temptation should be resisted, for a narrator represents a point of view, with selective responses expressive of its own nature. Every narrator, even the "objective" observer, must be understood to have a point of view, to see things from a certain angle and to be discriminating about what he or she chooses to respond to and to report.

When we regard Chamber Theatre as a way of dramatizing the style of a narrative text, we can see the possibility of relating the narrator to the action of the story and to the audience. Chamber Theatre uses stage movement to demonstrate the shifting relations of the narrator to the characters and to the audience. If we think of the external narrator as an agent in the scene, then his or her acts must be representative of some underlying characterological principle. Since the novelist does not specify acts, other than verbal acts, there is but limited opportunity for such a narrator to represent him or herself. In Chamber Theatre, however, the narrator is able to employ vocal inflections and nonverbal gestures which are inferred from the general laws of human personality and the social matrix which is the cultural model for us all.

From the standpoint of stylistic analysis, style is the "individual linguistic system of a work or group of works."[7] Leo Spitzer argues that the psychological characteristics of the narration can be inferred from the traits of its style on the assumption that a "mental excitement which deviates from the normal *habitus* of our mental life must have a co-ordinate linguistic deviation from normal usage."[8]

[7]René Wellek and Austin Warren, *Theory of Literature* (New York: Harcourt, Brace and World, Inc., 1949), p. 184. Reprinted by permission of the publishers and Jonathan Cape, Ltd.

[8]Leo Spitzer, *Linguistics and Literary History* (Princeton: Princeton University Press, 1948), p. 1-40.

When an author undertakes to create a fictive world we can usually expect that world to differ in some degree from the author's own social environment. True, there may be an autobiographical relationship between an author's life and his/her fiction, but if there were no differences then the work would be an autobiography. Inevitably there is some deviation. An author is perfectly capable of altering personal manner or style to suit the demands of a work. There is, of course, profit in studying an author's opus in relationship to biographical facts, but one should be cautious about identifying the author with the storyteller in the tale. The techniques of Chamber Theatre are devoted to the staging of a particular story with its particular storyteller and any relationship the narrator may have to the author must remain the concern of other literary studies. It is not that such studies are unimportant in themselves, it is just that they are irrelevant to the immediate concerns of Chamber Theatre. We are limited in the context of style to the habitus of the narrator's mind.

Chamber Theatre provides an opportunity for verbal and nonverbal expressions of the symbolic action which the literary text represents. In reading *Moby-Dick*, for instance, the qualified reader who is something of an act*er*, if not an act*or*, will at the very least make explicit verbal gestures when reading Captain Ahab's fateful words upon sighting the white whale: " 'There she blows! there she blows!—there she blows! There again!—there again!' he cried, in long-drawn, lingering, methodic tones, attuned to the gradual prolongings of the whale's visible jets."[9] Melville wants the reader to hear Ahab and to see the whale; if he can make the reader see the whale *through* Ahab, he will impress the reader with the kinship, the deep identity of Ahab and Moby Dick. So Ahab sings out, "There she blows!" in rhythm with the whale's spouting. Ahab's speech, therefore, is not merely an expression of the whale's proximity, but is itself a gesture in kinaesthetic imitation of Moby Dick. Melville uses language referentially, language that indicates the object, Moby Dick. He also uses language mimetically, providing a rhythmic analogue in sound to match Moby Dick's behavior.

In a Chamber Theatre production of Melville's novel, an actor would speak Ahab's words in a rhythm appropriate to the rhythm of the whale's spouting; *but without the narrator's narration*, an audience would not be aware of the timing of Ahab's speech with the spouting since it, of course, cannot see Moby Dick.

Melville had no physical whale either, so he had to provide a verbal description of the aural-visual correspondence in the narration. The language of the narration is not merely a discursive recognition of the rhythm of Ahab's speech and the spoutings of the whale, it is a poetic

[9]Herman Melville, *Moby-Dick*, Chapter 133.

expression of the kinship of Ahab and Moby Dick. Note the use of three strong successive accents in "long-drawn, lingering"; note the alliterative use of "1" and the use of similar vowels and similar consonants. In other words, the very language of the narration partakes of the rhythmic qualities of Ahab's speech; the rhythmic behavior of the whale inspires the rhythmic pattern of Ahab's speech, as well as the speech of the narrator. In a Chamber Theatre production the audience would receive the full verbal expression of these correspondences.

Style is the principal means by which literature dramatizes the narrator's point of view as it relates to the setting, the characters, and the action of the story being narrated. In Chamber Theatre the words of a literary text are more fully realized as gestures, and there is little danger of the narrative attitudes reverting to substitutes for action; there is, rather, a promise of advancing from preparation for action into action itself. Chamber Theatre guarantees the vitality of the symbolic nature of literature.

5

EPIC THEATRE

Wherever there is narration there is a story and a storyteller. In fiction the narrative element is readily identified, but in drama it is often concealed because the storyteller is disguised as a character and his/her story is generally brief: the Nurse in *Medea*, the Chorus in *Henry V*, the maid and the butler in nineteenth-century bourgeois comedies. Sometimes the major characters in a drama are required by the playwright to narrate a story: Mrs. Alving in *Ghosts*, Hamm in *End Game*. Some modern plays have taken to the use of narrators who are frankly identified as narrators: *Our Town, The Glass Menagerie, Ballad of the Sad Cafe, A Man for All Seasons, The Caucasian Chalk Circle*.

Bertolt Brecht, the author of *The Caucasian Chalk Circle*, has been a major influence on twentieth-century drama; as an antirealist he destroyed the illusion of realism by replacing the "fourth wall" with alienating effects that made his audiences continuously aware that they were in a theatre watching actors "demonstrate" figures on a stage who were narrating a story. He insisted on pastness, that is, audiences were not to be deceived into thinking that the events on the stage were occurring before their eyes here and now but that they were sitting in a theatre listening to a story whose action took place in the past and in another place. Erwin Piscator, Brecht's brilliant director, called this kind of theatre Epic Theatre because its fundamental method was narrative.

In Epic Theatre the "fourth wall" disappears and the actor or actress as narrator is free to make contact with the audience, to acknowledge its presence and to say, in effect, "What I am doing on the stage is for you, the audience, and for me, the performer. We are both interested in the character I am demonstrating and I will share with you what I have learned about my character moving among the other characters in this setting, wearing this costume, employing these props." It is possible in such a theatre for the audience to be moved by the conditions of the characters and at the same time to maintain a critical attitude toward the social, political, or psychological circumstances in which the characters find themselves. Indeed, it is the tensiveness[1] created by the audience's normal disposition to respond emotionally and the Epic Theatre's insistence that they respond critically that gives to the epic mode of Brecht's theatre its peculiar characteristic, its quality of "alienation."

It is not only the audience that is encouraged to maintain a critical perspective in the course of its aesthetic appreciation, but also the actor.

> At no point does he [the actor] allow himself to be completely transformed into the character. . . . He has only to *show* the character. Or, to put it better, he has to do more than merely *experience*. This does not mean that he must be cold when he portrays passionate people. It is only that his own feelings should not be entirely those of his character, lest the feelings of his audience become entirely those of the character. The audience must have complete freedom.[2]

For Brecht, the actor appeared on the stage in a double capacity —as actor and as character. The audience must not be allowed to ignore the fact of the actor's presence while he *demonstrates* the character. Seeing the intelligence of the actor at work, the audience is encouraged to exercise the same critical independence, for each respects the other's personal individuality.

Piscator required of his epic actors an "objective" style. They were to avoid empathic identification with their roles and to maintain a critical perspective. They were expected to create an "alienation-effect" by referring to the characters they were portraying in the third person, using the past tense and speaking the stage directions. The alienation-effect maintains for the actor a "distanced attitude" which allows him, in Brecht's words, to bring

---

[1]"*Tensiveness* is here preferred to *tension*, since the latter word often has about it an aura of distress, a feeling of anxiety. The word *tensiveness* includes this notion of tension but is much more comprehensive." Wallace A. Bacon, *The Art of Interpretation* (New York: Holt, Rinehart and Winston, 1972), p. 37.

[2]Bertolt Brecht, "A Little Organum for the Theatre," *Accent*, Winter, 1951, p. 28.

. . . forward his text, not as an improvisation, but as a *quotation*. At the same time it is clear that he has to render, in this quotation, all the undertones, all the concrete, plastic detail of full human utterance. His gestures, though they are frankly a *copy* (and not spontaneous), must have the full corporeality of human gestures.[3]

Whereas Brecht used these alienation devices in rehearsal in the hope that they would influence the performance, Chamber Theatre uses them in the performance itself. An audience at a Chamber Theatre presentation sees a narrator who uses the third person and the past tense speaking what might be stage directions with additional comments when referring to the characters in the scene.

A further application of the alienation-effect in Chamber Theatre is striking in its capacity to create distance and a sense of strangeness which alerts the audience to new values in an otherwise too familiar occasion. Suppose, for example, instead of the narrator, the actor playing the character speaks the following narration which refers to his character's action: "He seized his brother's shirt front and shook him, 'Don't ever say that to me again,' and flung him into a chair." If the actor speaks this narration with that emotion appropriate to the sentiments of the character's direct discourse, the audience experiences a curious ambivalence—is the *character speaking of himself* in the third person and past tense to suggest that he is *not* the character in the fullest sense, but simply referring to him and, in the direct discourse, simply quoting him? This degree of alienation need not be regarded as creating an atmosphere of indifference, any more than the umpire's or surgeon's distanced attitudes suggest indifference.

It is important to remember that "alienation" means not only the creation of a distanced attitude which makes "familiar objects to be as if they were not familiar," but also the carryover of this aesthetic perspective to social reality as well. "For a man to see his mother as the wife of a man," says Brecht in a note to "A New Technique of Acting," "an A-Effect [alienation-effect] is necessary; it occurs, for example, if he acquires a stepfather."[4] The social reality of the alienation-effect often uses the third person as a distancing device. A mother talking to her little daughter may say, "Mother doesn't want her little girl to do that," hoping, by the use of "mother" instead of "I," and "her" instead of "my," to depersonalize the relationship and so reduce the emotional intensity inherent in the scene. The depersonalization does not represent the mother's indifference toward her daughter but rather her great concern

---

[3]Bertolt Brecht, "A New Technique of Acting," trans. Eric Bentley, *Theatre Arts*, 33 No. 1 (January 1949), 39.

[4]Quoted by Hans Egon Holthusen in his essay, "Brecht's Dramatic Theory," in *Brecht: A Collection of Critical Essays* ed. Peter Demetz (Englewood Cliffs, N.J.: Prentice-Hall, Inc., 1962), p. 109.

for creating an atmosphere in which the little girl will *understand* that her mother, as a mother, has responsibilities for the protection of her children, and it is in this role that she speaks.

Robert Bolt, in the preface to his play, *A Man for All Seasons*, acknowledges a debt to Brecht and agrees

> that the proper effect of alienation is to enable the audience *reculer pour mieux sauter,** to deepen, not to terminate, their involvement in the play.[5]

Bolt is suggesting here that the audience, like the long-jumper who must move back from his mark a considerable distance if he is to lengthen his leap into the pit, must view the events on the stage from a certain distance that will eventually allow it to engage the events more deeply and with fuller understanding than if it indulged itself in slack-jawed wonder and sentimental identification.

This paradox cannot be demonstrated in print so well as it can on the stage, but the theoretical position may be illustrated thus: A character observes another character stumble and fall; he rushes to his rescue saying, "Look out, John," and then speaks an aside to the audience, "He always was a clumsy oaf," followed by, "Did you hurt yourself?" as he helps the fallen man to his feet. The quick aside to the audience increases the distance between the characters and reduces the distance between the character and the audience. The audience has been overhearing the characters in a "closed system" of relationships involving all the illusory devices of the theatre. When the character addresses the audience, the system of relationships opens up to include the audience and that is only possible if the audience now sees not only the character but the actor who is portraying him. The actor belongs to the theatre which the audience shares with him here and now; it is their natural habitat. When the actor returns to his closed system and as a character continues to speak to John—"Did you hurt yourself?"—the audience returns to the illusory world of the story with more assurance, more comfort, with a greater sense of belonging. The actor has taken them back with him into his imaginary world after acknowledging that he belongs, as the audience does and the characters do not, to the physical world of the theatre. The rapport now established facilitates the audience's understanding of the actor's relationship to the characters which, in Epic Theatre and Chamber Theatre terms, is that of a demonstrator.

Brecht himself remarked in a similar vein to Bolt's just quoted description of the alienation-effect:

[5]Robert Bolt, *A Man for All Seasons* (London: Heinemann Educational Books Ltd., 1968), p. xvii. Reprinted with the permission of the publishers.
*"to draw back for a better jump"

We make something natural incomprehensible in a certain way, but only in order to make it all the more comprehensible afterwards. In order for something known to become perceived it must cease to be ordinary; one must break with the habitual notion that the thing in question requires no elucidation.[6]

It is understandable, in view of Brecht's description of the paradoxical element of alienation, that he wished in his late years to have Epic Theatre rechristened Dialectic Theatre.

The tensiveness between critical objectivity and empathic subjectivity in a work of fiction precludes our settling at either extreme. As the narrator's position shifts under the influence of a dynamic point of view so does the relationship between empathy and alienation, between identification and demonstration. There is a continuum, a sliding scale of conditions observed by characters and narrators alike. If we follow the narrator in Nelson Algren's short story, "A Bottle of Milk for Mother," we see that he can be formally observant of *external* conditions:

> The arresting officer and a reporter from the *Dzienik Chicagoski* were grouped about the captain's desk when the boy was urged forward into the room by Sergeant Adamovitch, with two fingers wrapped about the boy's broad belt: a full-bodied boy wearing a worn and sleeveless blue work shirt grown too tight across the shoulders; and the shoulders themselves with a loose swing to them.[7]

He can also be formally observant of internal conditions: "Lefty paused, realizing that his tongue was going faster than his brain."[8] But the diction of the narration shifts from the narrator's formal style to Bicek's colloquial style when the narrator says: "Now, if the college-coat asked him, 'What big ten college?' he'd answer something screwy like 'The Boozological Stoodent-Collitch.' "[9] The narrator's adoption of Bicek's diction "screwy" suggests a degree of identification with the boy; the use of synecdoche, "college-coat," to refer to the cub reporter belongs to Bicek's mode of thought. Notice, however, that the spelling of "college" is formally accurate whereas the spelling becomes "collitch" in the boy's internal dialogue. The narration and, hence, the narrator is no longer completely disinterested; there is rather a degree of identification with the character to whom the narration refers.

If the narrator moves toward Bicek in a gesture of sympathetic

---

[6]Brecht, "A New Technique of Acting," p. 109.

[7]Nelson Algren, "A Bottle of Milk for Mother," in *Short Story Masterpieces* (New York: Dell Publishing Co., 1954), pp. 28-29.

[8]*Ibid.*, p. 31.

[9]*Ibid.*, p. 39.

identification, it is no less true that Bicek moves toward the narrator:

> The Lone Wolf of Potomac Street waited miserably, in the long unlovely corridor, for the sergeant to thrust two fingers through the back of his belt.[10]

It is not clear whether Bicek thinks of himself as the Lone Wolf of Potomac Street or whether that thought is the narrator's. It is clearer, however, that the narrator reports Bicek's misery while announcing his own response to the corridor as "unlovely." The final effect for the reader is a sense that the narrator shares Bicek's misery while Bicek shares the narrator's recognition of the corridor as unlovely.

Throughout the story the boy is never alone until the final moment in his cell when Lefty tells himself, "I knew I'd never get to be twenty-one anyhow."[11] However, the narrator is there—"Shadows were there within shadows"[12]—and it is consistent with earlier relationships between the narrator and Lefty Bicek that the boy's last speech is not only to himself but also to the narrator. Who are these shadows within shadows among whom the narrator finds himself? We have only to recall the quotation from Whitman that heads the story at its beginning:

> *I feel I am of them—*
> *I belong to those convicts and prostitutes myself,*
> *And henceforth I will not deny them—*
> *For how can I deny myself?*
>
> WHITMAN[13]

The answer, then, is that the shadows are the convicts and the prostitutes, while the narrator and Whitman are "of them." The narrator moves, in the course of the story, from a disinterested objectivity at the beginning to a full identification at the end when he becomes the "self" to whom the boy addresses his final statement.

It is an irony of history that Brecht's Epic Theatre, based on the principle of alienation, should provide the nexus for a theatre of involvement. The Living Theatre, and other theatres of encounter or confrontation, are anti-intellectual and depend for their theatrical success on their ability to assault the sensibilities of their audience. Brecht's theatre was meant to appeal to a critical audience; the theatre of encounter, whether intended as therapy for the actor or for the audience, prefers an uncritical audience. Nevertheless both theatres insist that the

[10]*Ibid.*, p. 43.
[11]*Ibid.*, p. 45.
[12]*Ibid.*, p. 44.
[13]*Ibid.*, p. 28.

axis of the theatrical dynamics run between the stage and the auditorium, thus destroying any vestige of a fourth wall.

AESTHETIC DISTANCE

To gain a different perspective of Brecht's principle of alienation let us start from a more conventional view of the "proper" apprehension of a work of art. In the early part of this century Edward Bullough suggested that there was a proper distance to be maintained in the face of a work of art to allow for a proper aesthetic response.[14] This ideal distance would permit the spectator to approach the work of art without having to take any utilitarian or practical action in its behalf but would not prevent the appreciator from becoming "involved" in the work. Though it is generally thought among sophisticated theatregoers that the spectator who is "taken in" by the stage illusion is provincially naive, it is Bullough's view that the ideal distance for maximum aesthetic appreciation is that distance which is just this side of a point or limen where the response threatens to become practical.

The use of the metaphor, "distance," to describe a complex aesthetic experience is apt to be reductive and misleading. The aesthetic experience is not linearly progressive, but dynamically interactive; it is compound and multi-leveled, instantaneous, and sporadic. There is in the epiphanal nature of the aesthetic experience a moment when there seems to be a double-distance. The character on stage raises a glass of wine to his lips and the audience accepts the glass for what it indeed is, a real glass; the lips, too, are real and even the impulse on the part of the character to pleasure himself with a glass of after-dinner port may be as real as such interior states ever seem, when they are the condition of another person.

So far, the reactions do not differ from the social realism or actuality with which we are all familiar. However, the audience "knows" the wine to be poisoned. In a social situation such "knowledge" would bring immediate practical action from the spectator. Theatre spectators, on the other hand, restrain themselves because they know the *stage* wine is *not* poisoned. Yet if the playwright has prepared this moment for an epiphany, or revelation of the transcendent truth that life and death are intimately related, the audience *must accept* the reality of the glass, the lips, the pleasure impulse, *and* the poison. Thus the audience refrains from crying out against the taking of the poison not only because it knows the wine is not poisoned, but also because it knows the "poison" must be drunk if the epiphany is to take place—that is, if it is to ap-

---

[14]Edward Bullough, "Psychical Distance as a Factor in Art and an Aesthetic Principle," *British Journal of Psychology*, 5 (1912), 87-98.

preciate the irony of the character's taking the wine, which in a symbolic sense is sacramental and life-giving, yet in a physical sense, poisonous and death-dealing. The epiphany may even include the realization that we must literally die in order to be spiritually reborn, and hence, the sting of physical death is transcended.

The transcendence which characterizes the epiphany, as James Joyce describes it—a sudden illumination "transmuting the daily bread of experience into the radiant body of everliving life"[15]—depends on the physical reality of the object which is transformed in this miraculous way into a symbolic significance. The symbol and the reality are mutually dependent. So it is in the aesthetic experience: the reality of the poison is intimated by the reality of the glass which is undeniably a glass, and by the reality of the wine which is undeniably liquid, though probably colored water. The point that must be reemphasized is that unless the audience accepts the reality of the wine, there is no chance for transubstantiation and hence no likelihood of an epiphany taking place. For the full effect of the irony, the audience must accept, too, the reality of the poison.

It appears then, that there are two orders of reality and two orders of practicality in operation; the actuality of the poison is of a lower order of reality than the reality of the effect, which is death, and the practicality of rescuing the character from that death by some form of intervention is of a lower order of practicality than that which restrains the spectator from ruining the epiphany by intervening. As for the death itself, the reality of which we must accept, it may be concealed from us by the timely descent of the final curtain, as in *Arsenic and Old Lace*, just as the elderly Mr. Witherspoon raises his glass of poisoned elderberry wine. In this case, the circumstances which might call for practical action are, by the descent of the curtain, snatched away from us beyond any hope of intervention.

DOUBLE-DISTANCE

For the actor, as for the director, there is a double-distance which concerns both of them as they interpret the scene. On the one hand, they are drawn toward an intransitive contemplation of the scene as one element in the larger aesthetic context of the complete work of art; on the other, they are drawn toward the concrete details of the scene's literal action. The director may be concerned with the practical stage problem of how to get the actor who drinks the poisoned wine into the beam of artificial sunlight shining through the window of the set. The actor may be con-

[15]James Joyce, *Portrait of the Artist as a Young Man* (New York: The Modern Library, 1928), p. 260. Reprinted by permission of The Viking Press, Inc.

cerned with practical matters such as how high to raise the glass before drinking, whether he should sniff the wine in appreciation of its bouquet or avoid that lest the audience be concerned with his discovering the presence of prussic acid through the smell of bitter almonds, whether he should turn this way or that so as best to feature the wine glass in the sunlight. These practical concerns with the objects of the scene constitute the "daily bread of experience" and cannot be considered apart from the aesthetic illusions, the miracle of transubstantiation, the irony of the death-dealing wine which is thought to be symbolic of the "everliving life." If we agree with Joyce that art is an epiphany, we must also recognize that the luminous radiance which characterizes the aesthetic pleasure derives from the tensiveness of the double-distance created by the dynamic presence of the physical object and the stasis of its aesthetic condition.

Double-Distance in Drama

It is often suggested by critics that the use of the narrator or commentator in the contemporary theatre tends to reduce aesthetic distance. Oscar Budel takes this view and supports it with references to Thornton Wilder's use of the stage manager in *Our Town* and to Tennessee Williams' use of the narrator in *The Glass Menagerie*. Budel says that in these plays the narrator is "at home in both worlds of stage and audience, and constitutes a suggestive link between the two realms."[16] It would be more accurate to say that the narrator here creates a *"double-distance."* When the audience arrives at the theatre for a performance of *Our Town* they see an empty stage in half-light with no curtain to conceal it. At this point, no aesthetic distance is established for no illusion of a real town is attempted. When a man enters the stage area with a hat on and a pipe in his mouth and begins to assemble chairs and tables, the audience accepts him as a "real" stage manager going about his "real" business. Aesthetic distance has been reduced to zero. But if we look at our program we will see that there is a stage manager listed in the cast of characters who is played by Frank Craven, whom we know to be an actor and not a stage manager. The "real" business of actors takes place on a stage, but now we see the actor as a character, the "stage manager." The aesthetic distance is beginning to increase. When the lights go down in the auditorium, the "distance" from the stage increases, but when the stage manager addresses the audience before the "play" begins, we find the aesthetic distance now reduced again because we, the audience, are recognized as a social reality and are taken into the fabric of the stage manager–stage experience. However, when the "stage manager" says, "This play is cal-

---

[16]Oscar Budel, "Contemporary Theatre and Aesthetic Distance," in *Brecht: A Collection of Critical Essays*, p. 74.

led *Our Town*," the aesthetic distance is increased with respect to the illusion of reality for we cannot accept the characters in *Our Town* as anything but fictions of an author's imagination. The aesthetic effect at the very opening of *Our Town* is of reduced distance with respect to the stage, the play, and the author, and the actors who are named by the stage manager in their own persons. Yet the stage manager does not identify himself as an actor by the name of Frank Craven. The effect of the distinctive treatment of the stage manager is to *reduce the aesthetic distance with respect to his character as stage manager* which seems so appropriate to what we see before us in the way of a bare stage and to *increase the distance with respect to his being an actor*, like the others whom he has just introduced.

After the first couple of sentences of the stage manager's opening speech, there are some notable shifts in the aesthetic distance: "the name of the *play*" gives way to "the name of the *town*," Grover's Corners, New Hampshire. A play is realistically appropriate to the stage and the distance is minimal; a town in New Hampshire is realistically inappropriate to the stage of the Henry Miller Theatre in New York, and in the absence of any illusion-producing scenery, the distance is maximal. The "stage manager" goes on to say, "The First Act shows a day in our town," thus expressing both *play* and *town* with both minimal and maximal aesthetic distance involved. The stage direction at this point reads "(*A rooster crows*)." Apparently somewhere backstage, out of sight of the audience, a record of a crowing rooster is being played on a turntable. Does the audience, now moving from the reality of the stage to the "reality" of Our Town, think it peculiar that there is a rooster in the theatre somewhere backstage, or do they find it natural that a rooster should be crowing in Grover's Corners in New Hampshire? No doubt there is some ambivalence; a tendency to laugh at the incongruity of a rooster in the theatre, and simultaneously a tendency to accept the "real" town which the "stage manager" now begins to paint verbally.

The relation between the actors and the characters and the audience in *Our Town* is more complex than our discussion has revealed, but enough has been said to make us realize that Oscar Budel is speaking too reductively when he flatly announces that the use of the narrator in contemporary theatre is to reduce distance. A more accurate analysis would reveal that the use of the narrator tends to increase the dynamic relationship between minimal and maximal distance as it affects the audience's response to the real actors and the real stage as one mode of existence and to the fictive characters, action, and setting as another mode of existence. It is not the contrast between these two realms, as each establishes its own peculiar distance at a fixed point, but rather the interaction of the two distances as they respond to each other; as one increases, the other decreases. It is the skillful use of this *interaction* which allows the playwright to establish a condition of reality for the fictional account he or she is presenting.

Double-Distance in Fiction

The contemporary novelist, J. D. Salinger, uses "double-distance" to create a special sense of reality in his work.[17] His "author" is associated with his "introduction" to what really is a kind of "prose home movie" and not a short story at all in much the same way that Wilder's "stage manager" is identified with the backstage character of the theatre.

The "author" referred to is the first-person narrator, Buddy Glass, who is, of course, a character in the story and not really the author, any more than Wilder's "stage manager" is really the stage manager of the Henry Miller Theatre. In Wilder's play we meet the players before we meet the characters. In Salinger's novel we meet the players in the "home movie" who are, to be sure, the characters, but Salinger gives them a life outside the story by presenting them as a "dissenting group" who, having seen the footage, disapproved of any serious plans to distribute the film.

The aesthetic distance for us as readers is reduced because we are able to meet the narrator as "author" and the characters as "players." Yet, because it is not a short story, a work of fiction, but a home movie, a documentary film, wherein the players are real, our aesthetic distance from the characters is reduced. The "author" is real, though a character in a fiction by Salinger; the "players" are real, though they are characters created by the author, Salinger, and not by the "author," Buddy Glass. A final instance of double-distance in the prefatory remarks presumably made by Buddy Glass, is the reference to Zooey Glass who will be seen in just a moment reading a letter sent him by his brother, Buddy Glass. The reference to Buddy Glass in the third person *by* Buddy Glass, the narrator, who speaks in the first person, makes for some ambivalence in the distance we are expected to maintain in our relationship to the "author" and his "players" as well as to the "narrator" and his "characters." The conclusion of the "preface" creates a narrative condition characterized by double-distance—(1) the distance involving the reader, Buddy Glass, the "author-narrator," and the "players"; (2) and the distance involving Buddy Glass, the "character," and the other "characters."[18]

It is the obligation of Epic and Chamber Theatres alike to stage the relationships between the dramatic and narrative elements in such a way as to demonstrate the thematic significance of the "alienation-effect" and the closely allied aesthetic effect of double-distance.

[17]J. D. Salinger, *Franny and Zooey* (Boston: Little, Brown, 1961).
[18]*Ibid.*, p. 50.

It is ironic and comic that we are freer in the illusions of art to face the realities we shun in everyday living. It is ironic and comic that our consciousness of self is more vividly and accurately revealed in the distorting mirror of art than in the clear light of our social reality. Self-consciousness is essentially a comic condition. In Epic Theatre, as in Chamber Theatre, the use of narrative devices contributes to that alienation which prompts self-awareness. There is a qualitative similarity between the comic condition produced by the "alienation-effect" and that irony which characterizes the comic means by which the self and the community interact—"As he turns to his audience of equals, the ironic clown transcends superior and inferior alike."[19]

Hugh Dalziel Duncan suggests that art supplies forms of symbolic action for thinking about social integration. But he suggests further that art should be studied in its comic forms. If art provides the comic means, the comic manner, for thinking about social integration, and if social integration is a matter of comic unmasking, or "alienation," as Brecht would put it, then we can pass over his injunction that we must not mistake the "dynamics of representation . . . for the dynamics of the matter to be presented."[20]

For Chamber Theatre, as for Epic Theatre, double-distance and alienation are essential elements in the final illusion of reality that these two theatrical forms establish. In other words, Chamber Theatre is not less, but rather more "real" for its reliance on alienation and double-distance.

---

[19]Hugh Dalziel Duncan, *Language and Literature in Society* (Chicago: The University of Chicago Press, 1953). See especially Part II.

[20]Budel, "Contemporary Theatre," p. 85.

6

FILM

Film-makers are in many ways freer than dramatists to control the point of view. They can represent human beings as giants or midgets, make them impressive or negligible by photographing them from above or below eye level; they can sharpen contrasts, lengthen or shorten time, provide extraordinary depth with light and shadow emphasis, distort images for psychological effects, or even multiply images to represent past and present in the same frame.

Because the novel employs many of these same cinematic devices, Chamber Theatre can profitably study the techniques of film making. The novelist, of course, creates images with language, whereas the film-maker creates photographic images, and so some differences between the novel and film must be accounted for.

In the conventional, legitimate theatre, the audience is fixed in its seats in the auditorium, forced to view the events on the stage from a fixed angle of vision. In a movie house the audience is also fixed in its seats, but its angle of vision varies with the motion of the camera. What the movie audience sees through the camera eye may be viewed from close up or from a distance, from above or below; the camera may be stationary, while the action takes place before it, or it may move with the action or against the action.

The Chamber Theatre audience is likewise fixed in its seats and the dramatic action it views is framed by the stage, but the narrator, like the camera, may view the action from many different angles. The narrator may move close to a character in order to give a close-up of a subtle facial reaction. The audience does not see for itself the slight quiver at the corner of the character's mouth; it is obliged to take the narrator's word for it, since he or she is the only person able to authenticate the action. The conditions in the Chamber Theatre, when the narrator takes the place of the camera, are similar to those that obtain in a film studio. The audience sees the action taking place on the lot or sound stage just as it would in a legitimate theatre, but it also sees the camera in action, dollying, trucking, panning, tilting, etc. On the stage in a Chamber Theatre production of the scene the audience would see, not the camera, but replacing it, the narrator in action.

The means of making films is, generally speaking, patterns of motions, whereas the means of making literature is language. How the means in both arts is managed is a matter of manner or style. Gerald Temaner holds that the manner of both film and novel is narrative. He says:

> We must not confuse the manner and material of the film by holding that the film is dramatic because it has actors in it. The actors provide gestures, which are materials for the film-maker who is "narrating" the story. On the other hand, many films do have a dramatic aspect in their use of scenes, in which the content is directly presented to us, but these scenes are usually juxtaposed in such a way as to make us feel the hand of a narrator at work. Frequently the story is presented by an omniscient third person who sweeps across time and space telling his tale and sometimes even commenting on the events (in *October* Eisenstein is commenting when he cuts from Karensky to a bust of Napoleon). In *The Savage Eye* the story is presented through one of the characters while in *Rashomon* many characters narrate. The viewpoint can shift even to the internal in film whose parts are scenes, as in *The Informer* where Gypo's state of mind is externalized by his visions. The use of inter-cutting sequences and flashbacks in the film offer the same flexibility of time that a novel has (John Dos Passos' *USA* was influenced by the film).[1]

When Gerald Temaner speaks of the film-maker "narrating," he puts the words in quotation marks, presumably to indicate that, unlike the novel, it is not a verbal narration. But later he refers to the film-maker as "an omniscient third person . . . telling his tale." The film-maker tells his

---

[1]Gerald Temaner, "Toward an Aesthetic of the Film," *New University Thought*, Spring, 1961, p. 58.

tale by showing images on a screen; the novelist tells his tale by showing images in language. In fiction as in film it is often difficult to distinguish showing from telling.

Perhaps consideration of a summary passage from Harry Levin's study of James Joyce will help to close the gap between film and fiction, which many critics insist on maintaining:

> Bloom's mind is neither a *tabula rasa* nor a photographic plate, but a motion picture, which has been ingeniously cut and carefully edited to emphasize the close-ups and fade-outs of flickering emotion, the angles of observation and the flashbacks of reminiscence. In its intimacy and its continuity, *Ulysses* has more in common with the cinema than with other fiction. The movement of Joyce's style, the thought of his characters, is like unreeling film; his method of construction, the arrangement of this raw material, involves the crucial operation of *montage*.[2]

Harry Levin's perspective looks from literature toward film.

André Bazin's view looks from film toward literature:

> . . . in the silent days, montage evoked what the director wanted to say; in the editing of 1938, it described it. Today we can say that at last the director writes in film. The image—its plastic composition and the way it is set in time, because it is founded on a much higher degree of realism—has at its disposal more means of manipulating reality and of modifying it from within. The film maker is no longer the competitor of the painter and the playwright, he is at last, the equal of the novelist.[3]

If our interest in the comparison of the film with the novel were leading us to a close examination of one or the other of these arts, we might rest content with vague similarities and unmarked differences. But our concern with film has to do with what it reveals of structural influences on the novel and vice versa. We are interested in Chamber Theatre, which shares with film the necessity for making manifest the inner life, and shares equally with the novel its reliance on language for developing and maintaining a point of view. For these reasons we must explore more fully the intimate relations of film and novel.

If we were to agree that film *must* be different from the novel because it is bound to the world of material phenomena while the novel is conditioned by language to operate in a mental continuum, we would

[2]Harry Levin, *James Joyce: A Critical Introduction*, p. 88. Copyright 1941 © 1960 by New Directions Publishing Corporation. Reprinted by permission of New Directions Publishing Corporation.

[3]André Bazin, *What is Cinema?*, pp. 39-40. Copyright © 1967 by the Regents of the University of California; reprinted by permission of the University of California Press.

ignore some psychological truths, and we would ignore them at the peril of our aesthetics.

It should be understood that a novel does not abstract from human behavior those principles which, when theoretically conceived, constitute a systematic philosophy. What interests the novelist, generally speaking, is the infinite variety of the social surface, the cultural patterns of human behavior which, when examined from a special point of view or when seen in a certain slant of light, reveal the primary data of human experience which is concealed beneath the social surface.

Hume marks the path of the novelist's pursuit:

> Those perceptions, which enter with most force and violence, we may name impressions; and under this name I comprehend all our sensations, passions, and emotions as they make their first appearance in the soul. By *ideas* I mean the faint images of these in thinking and reasoning . . .[4]

Hume further states that "every simple idea has a simple impression, which resembles it, and every simple impression a correspondent idea." The philosopher refines these ideas until the traces of impression are lost or buried so that, in essence, love becomes the ". . . ideality of the relativity of an infinitesimal portion of the absolute totality of the infinite being"—not a concrete image in the lot; whereas, for the poet who retains the link between the idea and the impression, "Love is a burnt match skating in a urinal."

It is significant, of course, that the poet and the philosopher both rely on language for their expression. Bertrand Russell says, ". . . as education advances, images tend to be more and more replaced by words."[5] This tendency is more fully realized by the philsospher as he moves away from impressions and images. The film-maker moves in the other direction, relying less on words than does the novelist and philosopher, and by strengthening the "faint images" that form the ideas of literature, makes vivid the impressionistic source of experience. Ingmar Bergman says that his ideas for films often start with "a brightly colored thread sticking out of the dark sack of the unconscious. If I begin to wind up this thread, and do it carefully, a complete film will emerge." The bright thread may be a "chance remark or a bit of conversation, a hazy but agreeable event unrelated to any particular situation, a few bars of music, a shaft of light across the street."[6]

---

[4]David Hume, *A Treatise of Human Nature,* Book I, Part I, Section I (London: Oxford University Press, 1949), p. 1.

[5]Bertrand Russell, *Analysis of Mind* (London: George Allen & Unwin, Ltd., 1949), pp. 155-156. Reprinted by permission of the publisher.

[6]Ingmar Bergman, "Introduction," *Four Screenplays of Ingmar Bergman* (New York: Simon & Schuster, 1960), p. xv. Reprinted with the permission of Simon & Schuster and Lorrimer Publishing, Ltd.

The brightly colored thread seen as a bit of conversation relates to what has been said about the novelist's interest in the cultural surface of life whereas the dark sack of the unconscious out of which the thread sticks is, of course, the primary data, the substance of the collective unconscious that lends the final significance to the external event. Henry James in his notebooks remarks again and again on the significance of bits of conversation, and other fragmentary social experiences which were the données for many of his stories. What Bergman and James did with these impressions was to polish the images they led to so that the ideas could be satisfactorily inferred and the thematic interpretations successfully directed.

Though Bergman denies the interaction of film and literature, saying, "Film has nothing to do with literature,"[7] Herbert Read says that those who deny the connection between film and literature are apt to misconceive, not film, but literature. They do not see literature's distinctive quality as visual. Read insists that the aim of literature is

 . . . to convey images by means of words . . . to make the mind see. To project onto that inner screen of the brain a moving picture of objects and events, events and objects moving towards a balance and reconciliation or a more than usual order. That is a definition of good literature—of the achievement of every good poet—from Homer and Shakespeare to James Joyce or Henry Miller. It is also a definition of the ideal film.[8]

The questions of similarities and differences between film and novel can be argued at greater length, and much more could be said about their mutual influences. Chamber Theatre sees in the cinematic qualities of the novel and the interpretative capacities of the camera an opportunity to increase the reader's responsiveness to the structure of the novel. The suggestion here is that the narrator in certain novels can be seen profitably as a camera, not, however, simply as an objective eye, impersonal and lacking any capacity for interpreting surface events.

Robert Gessner says that contemporary fiction is

 . . . significantly affected by three concepts so closely identified with motion pictures that they can be called cinematic: (1) the sharper visualization of description and narration at surface levels; (2) the increased manipulation of time and space . . . (3) the presentation of a clearer view of thought and emotion on the deeper levels.[9]

[7]*Ibid.*, p. xvii.

[8]Herbert Read, "The Poet and the Film," in *A Coat of Many Colors* (London: George Routledge & Sons, Ltd., 1947), p. 231. Reprinted with the permission of the publishers.

[9]Robert Gessner, "The Film: A Source of New Vitality for the Novel," Book Review Section, *New York Times*, 7 August 1960, p. 4. Copyright © 1960 by the New York Times Company. Reprinted by permission.

To illustrate his first concept, Gessner quotes a brief passage from Hemmingway's short story. "Cat in the Rain," which has three cinematic "shots," all pure cinema in the sense that "the eye tells almost all." Put negatively, the narrator or camera does no more than point to the woman, the window, the table, the rain, and the cat. Here is the passage:

> The American wife stood at the window looking out. Outside right under their window a cat was crouched under one of the dripping green tables. The cat was trying to make herself so compact that she could not be dripped on.[10]

The first "shot" establishes the woman at the window looking out. The second sentence is a "medium shot" which identifies what the wife sees, while the third is a close-up of the cat.

There is little here to suggest that the shots are anything more than cinematic and objective. However, if the technical demands of placing the camera are to be met, or, in Chamber Theatre terms, if the narrator's movements in relationship to what he or she is observing are to be staged, we may find subjective elements asserting themselves. Since it is probably true that a completely objective perception is impossible, it may well be that human manipulation of the camera will reveal subjective biases. It is no less likely that Hemingway's narrator will express a subjective view in adjusting the cinematic "shots" of the text.

Let us examine how the sharp visualization of this passage from Hemingway's story might be subjectively altered when realized cinematically and how it might therefore be seen as an interpretation of the wife's condition. At the same time we will consider the movement of the narrator in relation to the shots.

It would seem reasonable for the camera or the narrator to be in the room observing the woman as she looks out the window rather than outside the room, perhaps in the rain, looking in at her. Now if the camera or narrator stays in the room and moves only to look out the window to identify what the wife sees, there is a medium or long shot of the cat under the table. The cat, like the woman, is sheltered, looking out through the rain; there is a suggestion that the cat and the woman are circumstantially identified with each other. Hemingway refers to the cat as "she"; perhaps to encourage a correspondence between the woman and the animal.

In the third shot, the close-up of the cat, it is not clear whether the camera and the narrator are seeing the cat from outside the dripping edge of the table so that they and the cat are on opposite sides of the curtain of dripping water or whether they are under the table with the cat on the same side of the dripping water. The camera-narrator was *in*

[10]*Ibid.*, p. 4.

the room while the wife was looking out. Perhaps, to insure some identification of the woman with the cat, the camera-narrator should be *under*
the table *with* the cat while she is looking out. However, the cat is more
exposed than the woman, more threatened by the elements, and hence
more clearly in need of "compacting." The camera-narrator, first in the
position of the woman, safe, but now threatened in the position of the cat
suggests by the duplication of point of view that the wife may not be as
secure from the psychological elements as she seemed to be from the
physical elements.

If, on the other hand, the position of the camera and the narrator is
entirely neutral, outside the room and outside the table limits, favoring
neither position, then we must face the realization that the camera and
the narrator are in the rain, fully exposed to what the cat shrinks from
and the wife is sensibly safe from. The clear objectivity of such a point of
view is self-defeating; it leads the reader to exercise concern for the
camera-narrator and to that extent neglects the circumstances of the
wife and the cat.

It is not important here to settle which point of view suits the story
best, but simply to indicate that the close-up from inside has a different
effect on the reader or viewer from that outside the curtain of dripping
water. Hemingway does not specify clearly where the camera or the
narrator is, but in the reader's imagination a stand must be taken on such
matters if the cinematic techniques are to be fully appreciated. The
visualization in Hemingway's story is sufficiently sharp and appears to be
objective, but it is a virtue in film-makers and fiction-makers alike, that
they reveal the subsurface of experience by throwing a special light on its
surface.

Gessner's second concept, the increased manipulation of time and
space, sees in the novelist's use of flashbacks and crosscuts a cinematic
influence. The flashback, a cut to previous action, is a commonplace in
both literature and film. Melville's novel, *Benito Cereno*, for example,
opens with Captain Delano's capture of a mysterious vessel, *San
Dominick*, an account which occupies three-fourths of the story's length.
During the court trial that follows the capture of the mutinous vessel,
depositions are given by the crew and officers of events that preceded
the mutiny. This alteration of the chronology of events creates suspense
because for much of the story what happens during the struggle for
possession of the ship remains mysterious. Only the depositions can
throw light on these events. When all is explained there remains the
denouement which resolves the now-clarified relationship between the
captain of the *San Dominick* and the captain of the *Bachelor's Delight* and
so Melville returns to the present. Melville acknowledges the aesthetic
necessity for altering the chronological order of events and the use of the
flashback in a passage near the end of the novel:

Hitherto the nature of this narrative, besides rendering the intricacies in the beginning unavoidable, has more or less required that many things, instead of being set down in the order of occurrence, should be retrospectively, or irregularly given; this last is the case with the following passages . . .[11]

In a Chamber Theatre production the narrator provides an agreeable transition between scenes in a flashback because of his/her physical presence in both the here-and-now and the far-away-and-long-ago. There is no difficulty in accepting a scene as present when all the evidence suggests that the events are occurring now. What may trouble us is the feeling both in films and on the stage that what is remembered by a character is nevertheless present, though it is clearly something that happened in the past. We see and hear all that memory recalls with the same immediacy that characterizes events happening in the present. The difficulty is only apparent where memory is concerned, for all memory is in the present; to recall an event is to see it and hear it now and all that distinguishes it from present reality is that the recollection is imagined; and yet, like the reality, it is happening in the present. This psychological fact is mediated for the Chamber Theatre audience by the presence of the narrator in events both past and present, thus proclaiming that there is only a psychological distinction between the imagined or remembered past and the substantial and immediate present.

Such conditions do not pose any difficulties for the sophisticated filmgoer, for as Alain Robbe-Grillet, the author of *Last Year at Marienbad*, says, in the introduction to the printed text of the film:

> What are these images actually? They are imaginings; an imagining, if it is vivid enough, is always in the present. The memories one "sees again," the remote places, the future meetings, or even the episodes of the past we each mentally rearrange to suit our convenience are something like an interior film continually projected in our own minds, as soon as we stop paying attention to what is happening around us. But at other moments, on the contrary, all our senses are registering this exterior world that is certainly there. Hence the total cinema of our mind admits both in alternation and to the same degree the present fragments of reality proposed by sight and hearing, and past fragments, or future fragments, or fragments that are completely phantasmagoric.[12]

Since the image on the screen is always present whether it depicts a

[11]Herman Melville, "Benito Cereno," in *Short Novels of the Masters*, ed. Charles Neider (New York: Rinehart & Co., 1948), p. 122.

[12]Alain Robbe-Grillet, *Last Year at Marienbad* (New York: Grove Press, Inc., 1962), p. 13. Reprinted by permission of Grove Press, Inc. Copyright © 1962 by Grove Press, Inc.

scene that is past, present, or future, it is difficult to relate events with the same complexity that is possible in literature with its large vocabulary of tenses. In the novel the action is *actually* in the present and only *virtually* in the past, for though the past tense normally conveys past action, the novelist actually creates for the reader a moment-by-moment image of the action. For example, in the sentence, "She leaned toward him and whispered in his ear, 'I love you,' " the first two verbs are in the past tense and the third is in the present tense, yet in reading the sentence one does not separate them in time. In fact, the reader accepts the events as happening in the actual present because the image is created in the actual present, but the use of the past tense gives the sense of a *virtual* or "seeming" past, and this is the experience we have of memory. By "virtual" we do not mean that the experience is unreal; it is really perceived, but the image exists only for perception. "It is only visible, not tangible,"[13] as Susanne Langer puts it. A mirror image is virtual, a rainbow is virtual. The past in the novel is virtual, as the present in the drama is virtual, for the drama the past is actual since the actors have already rehearsed the play and what they say has already been spoken and memorized, and indeed, the spontaneous sense of repartée is but virtual, since both parties to it know how it will end, having already played it through many times. The "illusion of the first time" makes the drama an art of the virtual present, whereas the use of the past tense makes the novel an art of the virtual past.

Films have developed the technique of crosscutting to suggest two events happening at the same time or two simultaneous events happening in different places. The crosscut is sometimes called the "cut for simultaneous action." In films the classic chase allows the viewer to be at once with the hare and the hound by cutting sharply from images of the one to images of the other. It is only an illusion of simultaneity achieved by the rapidity of the alternation from one image to the other. In literature it is more awkward. On a simple level language tries to manage simultaneity: "Nero fiddled while Rome burned." Clearly these two events are simultaneous, but they are presented serially and despite the word "while" we meet the image of Nero fiddling before we meet the image of Rome burning. We are able to put the two events together only after we have met them separately.

The novelistic use of the crosscut antedates the birth of film, but not until the advent of the film was the technique so widely used by novelists. Flaubert used it effectively in *Madame Bovary* when Emma and Rodolphe are "talking dreams, presentiments [and] magnetism" while the voice of President Derozerays can be heard addressing a crowd in the

---

[13]Susanne Langer, *Problems of Art* (New York: Charles Scribner's Sons, 1957).

square where they are celebrating the agricultural show. Rodolphe is talking:

> "Thus we," he said, "Why did we come to know one another? What chance willed it? It was because across the infinite, like two streams that flow but to unite, our special bents of mind had driven us towards each other."
> And he seized her hand; she did not withdraw it.
> "For good farming generally!" cried the president.
> "Just now, for example, when I went to your house."
> "To Monsieur Bizat of Quincampoix."
> "Did I know I should accompany you?"
> "Seventy francs."
> "A hundred times I wished to go; and I followed you—I remained."
> "Manures."
> "And I shall remain tonight, tomorrow, all other days, all my life."[14]

Flaubert's use of crosscutting between two scenes does more than create the impression of two scenes taking place at the same time. Simultaneity is but the ostensible effect. A more substantial result is the creation of a monumental triviality by interweaving two lines of lesser triviality. We have here an example of montage which is the principal device of the film no less than of the novel for effecting a "clearer view of thought and emotion on the deeper levels."[15]

To say that the movements of the narrator and the movements of the camera are analogous is not meant to suggest that the narrator simply records, without interpretation, the events before him. In the hands of a creative director even the camera appears capable of interpretation, but the narrator, seen as a human being in the presence of other human beings (the actors portraying characters), is clearly capable of interpretation and interaction with the characters in the scene.

Let us consider how a filmic treatment in a Chamber Theatre production of the following scene from D. H. Lawrence's story, "The Horse Dealer's Daughter," demonstrates the interaction between the narrator as a camera and one of the principal characters, Dr. Fergusson:

> Below Oldmeadow, in the green, shallow, soddened hollow of fields, lay a square, deep pond. Roving across the landscape, the

---

[14]Gustave Flaubert, *Madame Bovary* (New York: Random House, The Modern Library, n.d.), p. 171. For a fuller discussion of crosscutting in literature see *Film Form* by Sergei Eisenstein (New York: Harcourt, Brace, 1949), pp. 10 ff.

[15]Gessner, "The Film," p. 4.

doctor's quick eye detected a figure in black passing through the gate of the field, down towards the pond. He looked again. It would be Mabel Pervin. His mind suddenly became alive and attentive.[16]

The opening sentence of the quoted passage is a long shot. So, too, is the second sentence, but now the shot is identified with the doctor's point of view (his "quick eye") and hence we have not only the camera's view of what the doctor sees, but a view of the doctor, too, which means that we are close to the doctor, but at a considerable remove from the figure in the landscape. Then the narrator (camera) identifies the doctor's action—"he looked again"—which is seen close up, but what he sees upon a "closer" look is Mabel Pervin. Now the figure is identified, which means that a middle shot is given to the reader as a result of the doctor's closer look. There is a subtle shift from the camera's (narrator's) view to the doctor's view in this passage, heralded not alone by the identification of the "*doctor's* quick eye" but by a shift in diction from the formal language of the narrator to the colloquial usage of the doctor—"It *would* be Mabel Pervin." It is as though we "*heard*" the doctor speak, and since we are already seeing with his eye, we are encouraged to identify even more fully with him. We are in an excellent position to accept the next sentence of the text: "His [the doctor's] mind suddenly became alive and attentive."

In summary, the camera movement is: (1) a long shot of the pond; then (2) a long shot of the pond with a figure moving in it and at the same time a close shot of the doctor; then (3) a close shot of the doctor's action of looking again, which is also a middle shot of Mabel Pervin. The final effect of the series of shots is psychological because the doctor does not move closer to the figure in the landscape when he looks again, he simply concentrates his attention while the *camera moves* in order to dramatize this new "alive and attentive" state of mind.

Now, let us consider a Chamber Theatre staging of the scene. The opening sentence is a long shot which does not yet take into account the presence of the doctor. The narrator will then occupy the center of the stage and will, for the sake of the example, be looking down right as though the pond were located in the auditorium beyond the footlights on the right side of the stage. The doctor is moving slowly from the left side of the stage beyond the range of the narrator's focus but looking generally in the same direction. In the second sentence it is the "doctor's quick eye" which shares with the narrator a recognition of a black figure passing through the gate (a long shot), but, since the narrator and doctor share the vision, they will be close together and, since the camera-narrator now acknowledges the doctor's presence, it would be advisable for the doctor to have moved directly in front of the narrator so that he can see the doctor's shoulder *and* the black figure. The next sentence indicates that the doctor has intensified his concentration in order to identify the figure. In effect, he narrows his gaze to eliminate distracting elements of the scene; let the narrator as camera, then, move closer to the pond for a medium shot, that is, move past the doctor right down toward the pond. The next sentence is indeed spoken by the narrator since there are no quotation marks to assign it to the doctor, but since the diction is local rather than formal it may be spoken by the doctor to the narrator who shares his inner life. In that case, the doctor can move down right to the narrator's back and say over the narrator's shoulder, "It would be Mabel Pervin." The final sentence concerns the doctor's mind and for the moment is dissociated from Mabel. To make this relationship clear, the narrator turns from focusing on Mabel, the gate, and the pond, to look at the doctor face-to-face. The narrator, then, will say to the doctor, "his mind suddenly became alive and attentive."

The dynamics of the action of the narrator and the doctor are these: (1) the narrator moves as a camera would in taking first an objective long shot of the pond, then a psychological shot of the doctor's recognition of the figure; (2) the doctor's realistic movement along the road and his stopping to examine the figure moving through the gate at a distance; (3) sharing interior speech with the narrator.

If this latter action of permitting the character to speak the narration seems unwarranted, let us consider what D. H. Lawrence does in this same passage in the next line. The narrator asks the question, "Why was she going down there?" The narrator is omniscient in this story and therefore must know the answer; he could only ask the question by assuming the doctor's condition of ignorance. In effect, it is the doctor's question and not the narrator's; the doctor, perhaps could say it as though addressed to some other part of himself or to the fates that rule destiny, or, more simply, to the narrator.

If further justification is needed for narrator and doctor sharing in a dialogue exchange, look at the passage some twenty lines further on. The narrator says, "Then he could see her no more in the dusk of the dead afternoon." This remark is followed immediately by a speech of the doctor's in quotation marks: " 'There!' he exclaimed. 'Would you believe it?' " The doctor now exclaims in his own voice for no one to hear but himself, the fates, or the narrator. Again the simple solution lies in encouraging a dialogue relationship between the omniscient narrator and the doctor.

The Chamber Theatre's use of cinematic techniques in staging this scene from "The Horse Dealer's Daughter" shows how valuable Chamber Theatre can be in any critical examination of the construction of a narrative work of fiction. The narrator's control of the scene and his relationship to the character in the scene are manifested in this filmic treatment of the action on the stage.

Staging Alain Robbe-Grillet's novel, *Jealousy*,[17] presents an heroic challenge to Chamber Theatre. The novel lacks plot interest, ignores character development, slights psychological exploration, offering instead endless minutiae of superficial details of objects and persons after the fashion of a candid camera.

A guiding principle in Robbe-Grillet's practice as a novelist is that we must learn to confront objects without demanding meaning or significance of them; it should be enough for us that they are *there*. The tedium of daily repetitions of sights, sounds, and actions is not to be avoided, but, rather, faithfully recorded. The novel must learn what the film already knows—how to reproduce the sensual surface of objects. Things need no longer be seen from a fixed point of view; as in the cinema, they may now be captured from shifting angles of vision. A successful staging of *Jealousy* would, then, demand a recognition of this cinematic quality.

Let us agree to "film" the novel, to create the illusion that the audience is watching directors, actors, and technicians at work shooting the scenario of *Jealousy* on a sound stage. The theatre is arranged in a square with open spaces at each corner; the lighting is supplied by spotlights on standards in full view of the audience so that they can appreciate the "backstage" or "offstage" effect characteristic of a movie set. The use of a "square" theatre emphasizes certain geometric features in the structure of *Jealousy:* a triangular plot set in a rectangular house whose porch columns "cast upon the terrace shadows like those of a sun dial, cutting time and action into slices"; a trapezoidal plantation with banana trees planted in quincunxes.

The story itself is simple enough—the husband, a plantation owner, grows jealous over real or fancied intimacies between his wife, A, and a neighbor, Franck. The first-person narrator, somewhat strangely, never uses the ego pronoun nor is he ever seen in action or heard in direct discourse. Yet it is gradually borne in on us that this narrator is, indeed, the husband, for we are told, for instance, that three glasses, filled and served to the duo by the houseboy are removed later, empty. It is clear that A and Franck have had but one drink apiece and therefore the only way to account for the third empty glass is to assume that the husband drank it.

The clinical objectivity of the narration makes it possible to assume

[17]Alain Robbe-Grillet, *Jealousy*, in *Two Novels by Robbe-Grillet, Jealousy and In the Labyrinth* (New York: Grove Press, Inc., 1965).

that film *technicians* may be at work on a scenario. On this assumption we will assign to each technician those parts of the narration which seem appropriate to his particular technical function: the scene designer will describe the setting; the costumer, the clothes; the lighting man, the natural or artificial light effects; the sound man, the natural and man-made sounds. The technicians will move freely about the set and sound stage, making direct contact with the actors, and carrying their scripts on clipboards, design pads, or in ring binders, and referring to them as though they are working from scenarios. When the scenes are in rehears-al or are being shot, the technicians will retire to peripheral positions. The script person, however, will be very much in evidence on the set, especially during the rehearsal of the actors, for this person prompts them, reminds the director of scene sequences, confers with technicians about their special concerns. He or she carries a manuscript at all times.

The *actress* playing the wife, A, and the *actor* playing Franck appear on the set as actress and actor speaking lines from the narration that can be construed as referring to "professional" interests. For instance, the costumer might say, "She appeared in the same dress" and the actress would add, with an interrogative inflection, as though checking out her understanding of what the costume should be, "but without a hat." The costumer would fill out the moment with an improvised answer—"That's right, no hat." So that there is no misunderstanding, let me repeat: Robbe-Grillet's text reads, "She appeared in the same dress, but without a hat," and the actress has added the interrogative inflection while the costumer has improvised her own reply. During the "takes" and rehears-als the actor and actress will assume the roles of wife and lover and speak the direct discourse provided in the script as well as the indirect discourse which they will speak with the conversational tone of direct discourse, that is, they will characterize the narration.

The *narrator* appears as the husband during the rehearsals and the "takes," though he never speaks in direct discourse (Robbe-Grillet pro-vides no direct discourse for the narrator) and is never directly filmed by the camera. Nevertheless his use of conversational inflections preserves the emotional tone of the scene and lends it an air of social reality. On the other hand, his use of the third person depersonalizes the occasion sufficiently to insure "alienation" so necessary to Chamber Theatre. The narrator often talks to the director about things that are happening outside the house, things that are not included in the shooting schedule; he also speaks of matters that suggest deeper motives than appear on the surface, thus acting as an "advisor" to the director.

When the narrator refers to his manuscript, it is to suggest to the audience that what it is seeing and hearing has already been "written." There is an inevitability about the progress of the story of which the narrator is very much aware. Whenever he puts the manuscript aside and appears to speak spontaneously it is to emphasize a level of nonliterary reality. The narrator creates three levels of "reality": (1) as an actor in the "real" shooting of the film; (2) as a husband in the "fictional" story of *Jealousy* which will eventually appear on some screen with all the illusion of "reality" appropriate to film experiences; and (3) as a "real" man whose jealousy transcends the film and the novel (scenario) of which he is a part as actor and "husband."

The *director* speaks that narration which describes the action of the characters. Such narration gives the effect of stage directions which are, of course, the traditional responsibility of the film director. Since actors, too, have some responsibility for their actions, the performers in this production are allowed to speak some of the narration appropriate to their condition. The director often refers to a manuscript as though it were the shooting script for the scenes to be filmed. In the course of directing scenes he or she may improvise speeches to express a technical interest in filming. Sometimes the narration that the director speaks is addressed to the actors as "characters" and sometimes it is addressed to them as "actors." Hence the director provides the audience with the dynamics necessary to create the illusion that they are watching a "real" filming of a "fictional" story, while the narrator is creating the illusion that they are watching a "fictional" story being abstracted from the "real" world in which his jealousy has its true being.

Briefly, this Chamber Theatre production serves to emphasize the novel's objective nature by "filming" it in a studio. The "reality" of the studio is intended to establish the "fictional" quality of the novel as being existential and phenomenal. Since only what takes place in the house is "filmed," it is hoped that those sections of the novel which are narrated but *not* "filmed" will take on the quality of "reality" by virtue of the overflow, the spontaneous excess, that cannot be contained in the rigorous formality of the "film."

7
STAGING CHAMBER THEATRE

ACTING AND DIRECTING

The behavior of the actor in Chamber Theatre does not differ significantly from that of the actor in conventional theatre so far as conventional dialogue and explicit behavior are concerned. There are, however, special conditions that obtain in Chamber Theatre that may disquiet the conventional performer. For instance, he or she may be called upon in Chamber Theatre to "demonstrate" as did the actors in the Brecht-Piscator Epic theatre. During rehearsals, Piscator created an "alienation" condition for his actors by sitting in the auditorium with them and questioning them about the behavior, the motivations, and the intentions of the characters in the play. In the conference the actors were expected to refer to their characters in the third person and past tense.

If, for example, the actor were playing the part of Wong, the water seller, in Brecht's *The Good Woman of Setzuan*, the actor's conversation with Piscator might go something like this:

PISC: Tell me what you know about Wong.

ACT: He was a water seller in Setzuan, and life for him was not easy, for when the water was scarce he had to travel long distances in search of it, and when it was plentiful, of course, he had no income.

PISC: Was he a bitter old man?

ACT: I don't think so. His feet were tired from hours of walking with a

69

heavy burden because it was evening when we first met him and he had worked all day. He was stoop-shouldered from carrying buckets of water on his carrying pole. . . .

Consider that the conversation of the director and the actor continues, exploring the character of the water carrier, until they approach the moment of the opening of the play when Wong appears before the gates of Setzuan: the actor continues to talk of Wong in the third person but now he begins to use the present tense.

ACT: Wong walks toward the gates (*the actor is now walking from the auditorium where he has been talking to the director*) sees the audience, sets down his buckets and clinging to his carrying pole as a prop or staff says: "I sell water here in the city of Setzuan. . . ."

From the moment the actor begins to speak *as* Wong he uses the first-person pronoun to refer to Wong and continues to use the present tense.

Piscator used the technique of discussing the character with the actor offstage in the third person and past tense in order to encourage the actor to see the character objectively, to study him, analyze him. Such an objective attitude developed, so Piscator thought, an "alienation-effect" that prevented the actor from succumbing to any illusion that he *was* the character. It was hoped that the actor would carry on to the stage sufficient objectivity toward his character to give his portrayal the qualities of a "demonstration." The actor would show the audience through demonstration what Wong was like, how he talked and behaved. The alienation-effect was expected to operate subtly by socializing the actor's performance, allowing him to perform for the benefit of the audience, and at the same time preventing the actor from undergoing a psychological displacement of his ego. The alienation effect allowed him, as well as the audience, to view Wong as a character in a play and at no time to be seduced into regarding the water seller as "real."

Rehearsal techniques employed by the Berliner Ensemble for establishing and maintaining the alienation-effect consist of a large mirror in the footlights, and photographers continuously shooting pictures during rehearsals to provide visual records for the actors to study later.[1] Such techniques seem at first distractive, making the performer self-conscious. To see oneself in a mirror for any length of time is finally to see oneself as a stranger. This is exactly the intention of these techniques—to make the commonplace, one's own figure, seem strange; in other words, to create the effect of alienation. Once an actress learns

[1]Kenneth Tynan, report of a visit to the *Theater an Schiffbauerdamm* in East Berlin printed in *Perspective*, June, 1962, p. 32.

to show her movements to herself, she can, with a director's eye, bring forward the character's words as genuinely as possible and indicate the character's manner of living as fully as her knowledge of human beings permits. Once an actor gives up the idea of transformation, he can bring forward his text, not as an improvisation, but as a quotation. During rehearsals, the actors are encouraged to speak the stage directions and to make comments in the third person. This practice

> ... brings two tonalities into collision in such a manner that the second (the text proper) is alienated. The acting, also, is alienated in that it actually happens after being expressed in words, after being announced. The adoption of the past tense places the speaker where he can look back at a statement. The statement is thereby alienated without the speaker's having to assume an unreal standpoint, for, in contrast to the listener, he has read the play through already.[2]

Brecht believed that feeling should be brought out, should become gesture. As in the oriental style of acting, an emotion should be given shape, strength, charm, etc. The actors should handle their motion-emotions as they visibly observe their own movements and so achieve the alienation-effect.

The current preference for acting which is "spontaneous," in the sense that the actors immerse themselves in the mood and attitudes of their characters, tends to distract the audience because the "illusion of the first time" encourages it to believe that what it sees and hears is impromptu and unpredictable. "Epic" acting, the style of acting recommended for Chamber Theatre, assures the audience that what it sees and hears is accurately represented; appearances are to be trusted and the actors and characters are separated so that the audience is allowed to see the artist at work demonstrating his or her character consciously and conscientiously.

The Chamber Theatre actor or actress finds it congenial to be a demonstrator because the narrative text is rich in commentary, description of action, verbalized interior thoughts and feelings, and it uses the third person and past tense. It is important for the performer to realize that his or her demonstration *repeats* something that has already occurred, but that the repetition is taking place now. The demonstrator imitates the actions of the characters and we judge the characters from these imitations. The imitations are appropriate to the tone of the characters but they are performed with a certain reserve, a certain distance. The actor/actress must remain a demonstrator; he or she must not

---

[2]Bertolt Brecht, "A New Technique of Acting," trans. Eric Bentley, *Theatre Arts*, 33, No. 1 (January 1949), p. 39.

neglect to comment that "he did this," or "she said that," nor must the performer let him or herself be transformed into the person demonstrated.

In staging the narration it is wise to conceive, first, of the narrator in the center of the stage, the strongest position. As prime mover, director and controller of the story, the audience regards the narrator as the master of illusion, setting the scene with "Once upon a time . . ." The narrator relinquishes the central position as the characters are called into being, they are allowed to speak for themselves in direct discourse and to behave under the illusion of free will. This pattern of action is schematic, a model, and not to be understood as suiting all occasions.

A narrator speaking in the first person may share the center stage with another character in the story:

PORTNOY: "I'm sorry," I mumble, my back (as usual) all I will offer him to look at while I speak, "but just because it's your religion doesn't mean it's mine."

FATHER: "What did you say? Turn around, Mister, I want the courtesy of a reply from your mouth."[3]

The narrator interrupts his direct address to his father with a narrative description which luckily allows him to turn toward the audience as he delivers it and so motivates the father's demand that his son "turn around" when he talks to him.

A third-person may also share the center of the stage with a character:

NAR: She said to herself, as she listened to his breathing,

MAY: "If I confessed to Daniel, he would understand that I was lonely and he would comfort me saying,"

NAR: 'I am here, May. I shall never let you be lonely again.' "[4]

The suggestion that May is talking to herself can be regarded with a degree of literalness by letting her address her direct discourse to the narrator, who answers her as though he or she were Daniel speaking. Daniel's speech is in single quotation marks because it is set in May's speech which is set off from the narrator by double quotation marks. Nevertheless, we sense from the punctuation that it is Daniel speaking, even though at this point Daniel is actually asleep. The narrator in this

---

[3]Philip Roth, *Portnoy's Complaint* (New York: Bantam Books, 1970), p. 66. Reprinted by permission of Random House, Inc.

[4]Jean Stafford, "A Country Love Story," in *Short Story Masterpieces*, eds. Robert Penn Warren and Albert Erskine (New York: Dell Publishing Co., 1954), p. 451.

passage serves the audience by letting them know that May "listened to his breathing"; serves May by being that part of her that can be called "herself"; and serves Daniel by speaking in his voice, "I'm here, May."

Inasmuch as an omniscient narrator shares the inner life of a principal character, that narrator will likely share center stage with the character. The actor or actress portraying a third-person narrator, however, may feel it necessary to maintain a corresponding physical distance from the performer playing the role of the character. Such a conclusion is no more justified than it would be to infer that a surgeon, who is not a close member of the patient's family should refrain from touching the patient's naked body, or that a psychiatrist, as an outsider, takes liberties in sitting beside a patient lying on the couch. The omniscient narrator may indeed enter into a dialogical relationship with the character:

(Father Furman is thinking about his housekeeper, Mrs. Stoner)
FATHER: She had her points. She was clean.
   NAR: Though she cooked poorly, couldn't play the organ . . .
FATHER: Still she was clean.
   NAR: She snooped.
FATHER: But not for snooping's sake.
   NAR: She overcharged on rosaries and prayer books.
FATHER: But that was for the sake of the poor.[5]

Father Furman, a priest, feels obliged to exercise his Christian charity by thinking the best of Mrs. Stoner, but, as a man, he seems not to be able to suppress his annoyance with her faults. The priest is caught in the struggle of good with evil: the actor who is playing the priest wears the familiar cassock, the sign of spiritual good will perhaps, and so this figure will champion Mrs. Stoner's good points; whereas the actor playing the narrator, who is infinitely adaptable, will, for the occasion, express Father Furman's dislike for Mrs. Stoner. The priest *and* the narrator, then, will share the audience's attention.

A special case of alienation is created when a character speaks his/her own narration, i.e., the narrative elements that apply to that character. Suppose a character has but one word of dialogue, "Darling," which she addresses to a man standing at the window, but the word is preceded by a narrative description of her action and her feelings. Instead of letting a narrator speak the description, it may seem advisable to the director to let the actress who says, "Darling," speak her own narration:

[5]J. F. Powers, "The Valiant Woman," in *Short Story Masterpieces*, p. 404. Reprinted with the permission of Doubleday & Co.

Though she danced up the long flight of stairs, she entered their room quietly, but the sight of Repton staring out the window, forlorn as a drowsy horse, overcame her and she rushed to embrace him, crying: "Darling."[6]

To let the actress speak her own narration may seem advisable on several grounds: the director may feel that there is an awkward delay in the action if the actress is expected to remain offstage until "she rushed to embrace him," and no less awkward if she appears onstage at the words "she entered" but must suspend her impetuous rush until the narrator has finished his description of Repton.

Assume, then, that the solution is to let the actress speak the narration. Suppose she enters stage left and swings around an upright post with a girlish, gay, dance-like abandon coming to a halt on "she entered" because she now sees Repton who is on stage right gazing out a window down left. She pauses in wonder at the expression on his face while she describes his appearance. Then she rushes to him on "rushed" and the words, "to embrace him, crying" will carry her across the room and finally, she will say her line to him, "Darling."

If the director finds this solution to be something less than satisfactory because it leaves the narrator with nothing to say or do, one solution might be to retain the character's behavior and to cover the awkwardness of her having to suspend her dash to Repton while the narrator says, "she rushed to embrace him, crying," by letting her say "Darling, darling, darling" while the narrator is saying, "she rushed . . ." Having to repeat "Darling" will intensify her emotion and if it drowns out the words of the narrator, nothing is lost because he only describes in words what we see and hear her doing.

It is difficult for the inexperienced to learn to listen while on the stage. He or she constantly feels the need to do or say something. In Chamber Theatre the performer often has to be silent and simply listen to the narrator. If the actress who plays "she" in the scene just quoted from "Fifty Pounds" feels uncomfortable listening to the narrator describe her actions while she performs them, she might be allowed in rehearsals to speak her own narration, so that she gets used to the timing of her actions and associates them clearly with the words of the narration. When she is comfortable, the narration can be given again to the narrator, and the actress, having externalized the narration, can now internalize it more successfully as she *listens* to the narrator.

In the conventional theatre the art of making exits follows set patterns. The absence of the fourth wall makes it necessary for exits to be

---

[6]A. E. Coppard, "Fifty Pounds," in *The Collected Tales of A. E. Coppard* (New York: Alfred A. Knopf, 1948), p. 526.

made to the left or right or more often upstage. To avoid turning their back on the audience, actors have adopted the convention of timing their speeches so as to make their exit upstage after turning toward the audience to deliver their last lines. This convention is so well established that playwrights frequently provide strong lines for exit lines. In Chamber Theatre the convention must be relaxed because novelists are not under any obligation to provide characters with good exit lines. They sometimes do because it is in their best interests, as storytellers, to make the moment when an important character disappears for the last time a climactic moment.

In narrative literature a character may simply drop from the reader's consciousness without having been given a formal exit. Consider this passage from Frank O'Connor's story, "My Oedipus Complex":

> "Why are you talking to Daddy?" I asked with as great a show of indifference as I could muster.
>
> "Because Daddy and I have business to discuss. Now don't interrupt again!"
>
> In the afternoon, at Mother's request, Father took me for a walk.[7]

In this scene there is no exit provided for the characters. The narrator simply shifts the time and perhaps the place. The conventional theatre is not without resources for this contingency—it may simply dim out or black out on the scene. In Chamber Theatre the same device might be used or, more likely, the narrator will move to another part of the stage to indicate that the current scene is ended and another time and place is about to be established. The narrator's move without a blackout or dim-out leaves the two actors who have been playing the child and the mother to abandon their characterizations and return to their full status as actors, waiting for the narrator to give them a new assignment. The virtue of this solution is that the alienation-effect becomes manifest by the evident shift from character to actor.

The ease with which novelists move through time and space makes for difficulties on the stage where the conventional unities of time and place are more strictly enforced. However, with the help of the narrator, the problems become capable of solution, as, for example, in this scene:

> I put my napkin down, moved my chair back slowly, stood up and went directly to my room and to bed, where I slept fitfully until daylight. I dressed and went downstairs to the kitchen where my

---

[7]Frank O'Connor, "My Oedipus Complex," in *Short Story Masterpieces*, pp. 352-353. Reprinted by permission of Random House, Inc.

mother, still at the table, sat with her head resting on her arm-
—sleeping, perhaps. I touched her gently.

In this summary of action and time a continuity is suggested, but it
would border on the comic if the first-person narrator tried to perform
the action in a literal sense. Since the principal actor in the scene is the
first-person narrator, he can control the action of the character with
conviction. Consider this solution: Mother is sitting at the kitchen table;
the boy speaks his narration as he slowly rises from the chair, but instead
of going upstairs to bed, he slowly walks to his mother's side of the table
as she slowly rests her head on her arm on the table. The boy's action and
the mother's are coordinated so that they are complete by the time the
narration says, "I touched her gently." In other words, the boy rises and
goes to his mother while she rests her head, but the narration tells us
that, between the time of rising from the chair and the touching of her,
he has been to bed, slept, and dressed, and come down to the kitchen
again. The storyteller has, through the magic of language, compressed
time and space in order that the story might hasten along. The staging
respects this magic.

One further problem that actors in Chamber Theatre sometimes
find difficult is that of simultaneous speech. A third-person narrator may
summarize, for the sake of compression, what a character is saying in full
to another character in the scene. Since the conventional theatre has a
low tolerance for two people speaking at once on the stage, the actor's
tendency is to mouth in silent pantomime what the narrator is reporting
to the audience. Unfortunately, nothing attracts attention more strongly
than someone speaking what we, the audience, cannot hear. Conse-
quently, the effect is just the reverse of that intended. D. H. Lawrence
presents the actor with this problem in his short novel, *The Fox*. A young
man has come to visit two women, Banford and March:

> The youth was very pleased. He had eaten and drunk his fill.
> Banford began to question him. His name was Henry Grenfel—no
> he was not called Harry, always Henry. He continued to answer
> with courteous simplicity, grave and charming. March, who was not
> included, cast long, slow glances at him from her recess . . .
>   At last the talk dwindled. The youth relaxed his clasp of his
> knees, pulled himself together a little, and looked round.[8]

The performers playing Banford and Henry could hardly be expected,
through this narrative passage of some twenty lines, either to pantomime
their conversation or to sit in motionless silence. The most satisfactory

[8]D. H. Lawrence, "The Fox," in *Short Novels of the Masters*, ed. Charles Neider (New
York: Rinehart & Co., 1948), p. 591. Reprinted by permission of The Viking Press, Inc.

solution would be for them to improvise their conversation, permitting the audience to catch the drift of the exchange. Meanwhile the narrator observes the scene from March's recess, since it is her interior responses to Henry that form the bulk of the passage. Remember, too, that the narration and the conversation need not be continuously simultaneous. The passage is long enough so that the narrator, taking in the scene from March's point of view, can remain silent for a moment or two while the audience listens to the improvised conversation. Or Banford and Henry can suspend their dialogue for a moment while we listen solely to the narrator.

There is little to be gained in enumerating the problems encountered in acting Chamber Theatre productions; each scene demands its own unique treatment. However, suffice it to say that the differences between acting in the conventional theatre and in Chamber Theatre are not categorical, but relative.

SCENERY

Epic literature is characterized by a multiplicity of settings for the action of the story. Aristotle recognized the tendency of drama to limit, and the disposition of epic to proliferate, the number of settings. At first glance, then, the difficulty of staging all the many scenes of a novel in Chamber Theatre, would seem insurmountable. Especially so when we think of the detailed realism that both movies and the conventional stage have taught us to expect. However, there is also a tradition of stripped realism, selective realism, space staging, and simplified setting that exists in the theatre of the Western world. It is inconceivable that Shakespeare expected anything like full realism in the settings for *Antony and Cleopatra*. A modern editor identifies the setting in a single line of type beneath the cast of characters: *"Scene: In several parts of the Roman Empire."* A street in Rome is the setting for the congress of three men and the scene is but ten lines long. It represents but a pause in the movement of the characters from one private place to another via the public way. There is no dramatic necessity for a detailed representation of the street; if Shakespeare had thought there was such a necessity, he might have provided a verbal description.

It is much the same with Chamber Theatre. Since the fiction writer has no facilities for physical effects he must depend entirely on verbal descriptions. And while it is true enough that the word may be a poor substitute for the thing, there are occasions when the skillful management of words will conjure up images more satisfactorily than the stage or the film studio with all its sophisticated resources. Consider, for example, how difficult it would be to approximate in either of the other modes the "flannel fog" described by John Steinbeck in *The Grapes of Wrath*.

It would seem, then, that the best kind of setting, speaking generally, for Chamber Theatre productions, is the kind that has a minimum of standard, generalized pieces that can be fleshed out with detailed verbal descriptions provided by the author's text. Scenery for Chamber Theatre is less a painter's or decorator's art than it is a sculptor's art. The free forms of sculpture, or the more conventional structural elements of our environment, provide the best setting: ladders, stools, benches, platforms, ramps, pipes, etc. These structural forms have a nonspecific character that allows them to serve as elevation, separation of the stage into areas, centers of action, concrete objects of sufficient rigidity and physical resistance to permit the actor to use them freely without fear of exposing them as something artificial. If, for example, a prison cell is represented in the text, it might be well to represent it on the stage with an iron pipe screwed upright into a metal plate bolted to the floor and secured at the top by an iron elbow fixed to the inner face of the proscenium arch. A bench furnishes the cell. Now the actor can freely beat on the iron pipe if he would so express his anguish at imprisonment. He can kick the pipe with authentic viciousness as though it were the unfeeling stone of his cell. He can cool his fevered brow on the cold iron of the pipe and receive a sensation similar to that provided by the verbal description of the cold stone in the text. If his back itches, he can seek relief by rubbing it on the iron pipe with all the energy appropriate to his need. None of these effects can be so readily achieved with painted, canvas-covered flats.

Though structural, functional elements serve the needs of the multi-settings of fiction very well, there is also a place for screens or panels that serve by their coloring, their texture, or their decoration, to provide a setting with the proper tone. A story may depend heavily on the historical character of its settings. A luxurious hanging properly draped (for the historical period represented) and an appropriately elegant chair of the same period may be enough to establish the right quality for the performance. If screens are used, it is best to rely heavily on the texture of the material used to cover the screen frames; next in importance are the colors and patterns applied to the screens' surfaces.

Arena stages and thrust stages, rather than proscenium stages, offer the best relationships of the performers to the audience and the text of a Chamber Theatre production. It is significant, perhaps, that these stages discourage the use of scenery, especially of the conventional painted canvas variety. The open stages of James Miller use standing scenery which is essentially structural and therefore good for Chamber Theatre. Miller's stages often have a permanent cyclorama upon which projections can be cast. This type of scenic background is very flexible and ideal for the generalized effect frequently demanded by a Chamber Theatre text.

LIGHTING

Lighting can, because of its enormous flexibility and efficient control, be extremely useful in producing Chamber Theatre. Illumination is, of course, the first concern, but beyond that is the value of establishing acting areas in order to make swift transitions from scene to scene. Sometimes the action may rapidly alternate between two scenes, and it would be comically awkward for the actors to enter, exit, and reenter in rapid succession. In such cases it is simpler, and perhaps more effective, to dim out and dim in the alternate settings. The rate at which one dims out a scene ranges from a slow fade to a sudden blackout, and to each is attached a different emotional value which contributes immensely to the effectiveness of a scene.

One valuable and special use of lighting in Chamber Theatre concerns the relationship of the narrator to the character. It sometimes happens that a character's being alone is important to the significance of a scene. The narrator's presence on the stage, may reduce the effectiveness of the character's isolation. Skillful lighting, however, can include the narrator in the scene without destroying the isolation of the character. When the narrator does interefere, instead of staging a deliberate exit in full view of the audience, he or she can be eased into the shadows by narrowing the beam of light to feature the character and momentarily cast the narrator into the shadows.

Occasionally it is necessary to feature the narrator who may be expressing an observation too subtle for the consciousness of the character. The light that served to illuminate narrator and character may be narrowed to set off the narrator from the character who is now in the shadows. It relieves the necessity for the character to make a complete exit since he or she will be needed in a moment to share the scene with the narrator again, in which case the area of light has simply to be widened again to include the character.

Finally, lighting can be very helpful in establishing mood. Unlike scenery, which tends to particularize and therefore to compete with the spoken descriptions in the text, lighting is highly generalized and operates subtly and often indirectly on the senses. A cold, dreary light on the stage will support any particularized description of a cold, dreary atmosphere expressed in the text. Of course, it can be used in a realistic fashion to represent sunrise or sunset, or to suggest lightning, but its greatest value is the creation of moods.

Brecht, who was a complete man of the theatre, had theories about

lighting that may well serve Chamber Theatre. He felt that it was important to show the lamps that provided the stage lighting in order to
prevent any unwarranted illusion that the light had any other source
than that of stage lighting equipment. He said:

> If we light the acting in such a way that the lighting equipment
> is seen by the spectators, we destroy a certain amount of their
> illusion to be witnessing an actual, spontaneous, unrehearsed
> event. They will realize that pains have been taken to show some-
> thing, to repeat something under particular circumstances—as, for
> example, in very bright light.[9]

Brecht's suggestion is but a further example of alienation.

COSTUMES

Costumes are intimately related to character, serving by physical extension to express either individuality or historical authenticity. In the
theatre, costuming takes its importance from the fact that a character is
completely and continuously in view while on stage. In a novel, the
narrator can select certain expressive elements of dress and suppress
references to the remainder of the character's costume. Traditionally,
we demand full costuming in the theatre, but selective costuming will
generally serve the needs of a novel. Having a full view of the actor
seems to demand a fullness of costume, whereas the necessity for serial
presentation in the novel of the details of dress, which must be "added
up" by the reader, creates the potential for boredom. The theatre tends
to encourage full dress, while the novelist economizes and selects with
great care those elements that best "reveal" character.

Designing costumes for Chamber Theatre presents some difficulties. The visual demand for a complete costume must not obscure the
narrative prerogative of selective detail. Some authors say almost nothing about the dress of their characters, hence the designer is free to
exercise his/her own judgment. If the author's description is
impressionistic—"When she entered the room one was conscious only of
lace"—it is wisest to apply the impressive detail to a basic costume which
offers nothing to distract from the main impression. In the case under
consideration, it might be advisable to add to a plain, undecorated dress,
a jabot of billowing lace at the throat. If, on the other hand, the author's
account of the impression waxes somewhat more detailed—"When she
entered the room one was conscious only of lace: lace at the throat, lace

[9]Bertolt Brecht, "Der Buhnenbau des Epischen Theaters," reprinted in an English
translation in *World Theatre*, 4, No. 1—*The Actor* (Winter, 1954), 21.

at the wrist, a flash of lace beneath her skirt, and finally, lace stockings"—then the designer may feel obliged to dress the character in lace collar, lace cuffs, lace petticoat, lace stockings.

If the author's description of a costume is highly generalized—"She was gaudily dressed"—the designer may wish to dress the character in clothes that will reflect gaudiness in every detail, but if the other characters have been costumed in a basic dress to which characteristic elements have been added, he or she may prefer to express the gaudiness by simply adding an enormous multi-colored artificial flower at the waist of the costume, which is otherwise a simple basic dress.

Since characters in a novel may move quickly from scene to scene, it is probably practical to demand costuming realistic in every detail. Selectivity, in this case, is not determined by the nature of the verbal description but rather by the brevity of scene transitions.

Let us suppose at the conclusion of a scene in a woman's apartment the narrator says,

> She hurried through the noon traffic crosstown to her office where she spent the afternoon balancing her checkbook, rummaging through old letters, and gazing out the window. The four o'clock whistle woke her and she hurried back through the crowded streets to her apartment.

Here is a brief scene in an office sandwiched between two very brief scenes that are themselves transitions from and to the woman's apartment. Let us suppose that she is dressed suitably for both scenes. Since nothing is mentioned in the text about a change of costume, all that may be necessary to effect a recognition of indoors and outdoors would be for the woman to pick up her purse and a pair of gloves, which she does not have to put on, as she leaves one side of the stage, her apartment, and crosses to the other side of the stage, her office. She appears ready for office work the moment she puts her purse and gloves on the desk. She may continue to stand as she rifles through some random papers on her desk and then gazes out what is identified in the text as a window. After a considerable pause, the narrator shocks her into activity by saying, "The four o'clock whistle woke her." A slight pause as she picks up her purse and gloves, then she recrosses the stage to her apartment.

Suggestive costuming is recommended for characters normally identified by their uniform. A performer may very well play more than one such character in a Chamber Theatre production, and it is convenient when only a partial change of costume is required. But more important is the alienation effect produced by such partial costuming. To wear a policeman's badge on a business suit, or to put on a butcher's apron over a business suit, is to shock the audience into a recognition of the policeman's authority and the butcher's bloody business by inappropriately relating them to the businessman.

The problems of costuming a narrator who is a character in the story are no different from those that apply to other characters. But if the narrator is outside the story, then special considerations must be faced. The costume, like the performer's speech and behavior, should be congruent with the style of the narration. Third-person narration is generally formal, except for those moments when the narrator alters his diction to suit the tone and attitude of the character with whom he is empathically engaged. Thus, his or her costume should be formal in the degree that is appropriate to the characters in the story when dressed for formal occasions. However, if the story concerns Indians on a reservation, or sailors on an old tramp steamer, or share croppers, formal dress for the narrator would be out of place. Less conspicuous uniforms than the tuxedo may also suggest a somewhat formal occasion.

If, as in *Tom Jones,* the narrator speaks from a contemporary point of view shared by the characters and the author, then the costuming of the narrator will not differ essentially from that of the characters. If, however, the author has created a modern narrator, speaking in a modern idiom but recounting a story set in an earlier time, there will be a corresponding disparity in costuming.

Similar problems arise in the case of modern translations of classics. A present-day translation of *The Iliad* and *The Odyssey* employs a twentieth-century diction which lends a contemporary aura to the texts. A Chamber Theatre production of these texts would be well-advised to use costumes consistent with the language of the translation; the soldiers' uniforms, for example, should be modern rather than ancient. The translator clearly intended to create an atmosphere to which the twentieth-century reader could relate with more immediacy. Echoing the diction by using modern costumes merely strengthens this response.

Consistency is the watchword in costuming Chamber Theatre productions. Look to the literary text itself for guidelines. Be sure that the costumes and other features of the setting support the tone, the mood, the theme, the diction, the style, etc., of the text. Generally speaking, suggestive costuming and settings serve the needs of Chamber Theatre best. The more selective the elements are, the better the director can control the emphasis of the production. The simpler the designs, the more efficiently the alienation effects can be achieved. The bolder the concept of the lighting, setting, and costuming, the more certain the director can be of its effect on the audience.

HAND PROPS

Like costumes, hand props are often an extension of the body, and a performer can make excellent use of them to express the character he or she portrays. A whip, a cane, a billiard cue, a gun are all extensions of the human hand and arm, and their physical presence in the actor's hand makes clear the nature of the extension, but the importance for the actor is the opportunity they afford for developing behavior patterns that express the nature of the character who employs these extensions. The actor's management of a cane, for instance, will quickly show an audience that the character needs it for a prop in his feeble condition, or that he is a boulevardier of the late nineteenth century, using it to express the quality of an elegant gentleman.

Hand props are serviceable in Chamber Theatre because they are at once more available and more easily disposed of than settings or costumes. A performer can pick up a prop from a table and use it as long as it is functional in the scene and then when the scene changes, she can replace it on the table and it quickly disappears from the audience's consciousness.

It is a comfort to actors to be able to use *actual* hand props. The performers can elaborate the use of the prop if it exists for them in concrete form. It has its own continuity when it is real and does not have to be revitalized for the audience as do imaginary hand props. Nevertheless there are times when it is advantageous to have imaginary hand props, and set props. If there is a brief moment in a scene when a character sits down to an old upright piano and bangs out an old sentimental tune, it is aesthetically economical for the actor to sit down to a table and pantomime the finger action. The use of the actual table for the imaginery piano gives the performer the advantage of something physical to work with but also allows him or her to face the audience so that it can see both the character's facial expressions and finger movements. If a real upright were used, the performer could not face the audience directly and his/her fingering would be realistically constrained rather than imaginatively released.

Frequently it is best to have a completely imaginary prop with no physical basis at all. If a character picks a flower of rather exotic description provided by the text there is little need for reproducing the flower in some concrete fashion, especially if its only importance to the scene is the fact that it contains at its heart a large black and gold bee which crawls slowly out of the flower and onto the character's finger. In his fascination with the bee, the character drops the beautiful flower which now lies neglected on the grass and is never recovered. If a physical prop for the flower is used, it must be disposed of. It is unlikely that the text will provide for the removal of the flower when the scene changes. Playwrights must be careful about such matters, but the novelist is freer of such constraints.

The mixture of physical props with imaginary ones creates aesthetic problems that are not easily solved by any appeal to aesthetic laws.

Often the problems will present themselves in commonsensical terms and their solutions will very likely be in the same terms. To drop a real letter into an imaginary mailbox may distress an audience as it sees the letter flutter to the stage floor where no mailman is ever likely to see it. The solution may be to retain the real letter since it serves the character so well in the expression of his personality and let him post it offstage where the audience is willing to grant that an equally real mailbox exists.

On the other hand, there is no aesthetic difficulty in using a real fly swatter to kill an imaginary fly. The fly is so small that the audience cannot see for itself whether there is, or is not, a real fly on stage. Yet the use of a real swatter recommends itself because the *way* in which the character uses it may be expressive of his mood and temperament.

Nor would it be difficult to decide that no physical props should be used in the climactic scene of D. H. Lawrence's *The Fox*, when the young man, crouching in the dark, shoots the fox as he approaches the hen house. To use a real shotgun without really firing it seems unconvincing. If one decides to fire the gun with a blank charge and risk deafening the audience, then one must consider whether a real fox is needed. The fox in the fiction is killed by the shot and the examination of the beautiful creature in death, with its magnificent fur and strange, musky odor, etc. has a profound effect on the heroine. These circumstances dictate against the fox being offstage, like the mailbox, and *presumed* to be actual; it would mean that the heroine's examination would have to be offstage and reported to the audience indirectly. This will not do. No better solution is afforded by having the young man who is offstage shoot a real or imaginary fox which is onstage. The scene demands that the young man, the gun, and the fox, all be onstage. We are left with the solution of making fox and gun imaginary and keeping the action onstage. Fortunately, the situation is saved somewhat by Lawrence's excellent description of the fox. We are allowed to see more than just the inert figure of a dead animal, we are allowed to see the fox as the heroine sees it.

If there were a real fox, there would be too many possibilities for the real animal to appear other than the way the heroine sees it. The absence of the real gun is harder to excuse, because the text makes much of the loud report of the gun and the noisy disturbance in the barnyard caused by the blast. Yet something can be done to ease the awkwardness: (1) place the young man down left facing up right so that his body conceals most of the gun as he holds it to his right shoulder, thus concealing from the audience any clear recognition of the gun as real or imaginary; (2) place the narrator up right and have him or her move slowly toward the young man and up the ramp of the hen house, while describing the action of the young man and the fox in the dark. The narrator's low voice and slow movement in imitation of the fox will tend to "realize" the actual fox for the audience. Then Lawrence says, ". . . there was the awful crash of the gun . . . as if all the night had gone smash. . . ." The narrator suddenly arrests his movement and raises his voice sharply on such words as "crash" and "smash."

Three things have been done in the staging here to compensate for losses of reality made necessary by the deeper requirements of imaginary props (fox and gun). First, the young man has been so placed as to partially conceal the gun so that the question of its being actual or imaginary is not forced on the audience. Second, the real narrator is put in the position of the imaginary fox and moves with the fox's tempo up the imaginary ramp of the imaginary hen house where the real young man crouches with his imaginary (?) or real (?) gun. The placement of the narrator and his movement tend to "realize" the fox. Third, the sudden shift in volume and tempo of the narrator's speech when the gun is fired and the night is filled with the gun shot, the squawking of ducks, the stamping of the pony, and the fowls "scuffling and crawking" provides a sound level that "suggests" the reality of the "crash" of the gun and the subsequent noises of the yard.

No principles have been devised that will solve all the problems of staging a Chamber Theatre production of a novel. Awkwardnesses occasioned by putting on the stage what was conceived for the printed page cannot always be eliminated or alleviated. Thirty years of experience staging fiction in Chamber Theatre has convinced this author that the transfer of narrative literature from the printed page to the stage will always necessitate some arbitrary solutions, misrepresentations, and suspect rationalizations. But, perhaps, the reader does not need to be reminded that the ideal has yet to be achieved in any art. Despite the inevitable compromises and distortions that threaten the original text when staged, they are no more destructive than those faced by the director of a play. It is not profitable to make too much of these difficulties, but it is no less important to recognize them than it is for the navigator to beware reefs and shoals. They are there and must be faced, then circumvented.

However, there are important gains in Chamber Theatre that more than compensate for the losses. When a story is actualized on the stage, the audience is made more vividly aware of the dynamics of literary structure and becomes more responsive to imaginative content and more critically sensitive to theme and mood.

PREPARATION OF THE TEXT

The assumption here is that the director is also the adapter of the novel or short story for production. The admonition that should govern the adapter's decisions is "don't": *don't* cut anything unless, for the sake of the "two hour traffic of the stage," you must abbreviate the original text; *don't* rewrite unless you absolutely have to, as in the case of easing transitions where your cutting has created an awkward seam; *don't* cut the descriptions just because they are descriptions; *don't* change the indirect discourse to direct discourse; *don't* alter the diction in the interest of "clarifying," "modernizing," or "dramatizing" the style. The list of "don't's" is long because adapters have no one to answer to but themselves and they are apt to grow injudicious, drunk with power, and quickly begin to think of the work of fiction as theirs rather than the author's. A good rule to follow in adapting fiction for Chamber Theatre is this: If a great deal of cutting is necessary, if there really is a lot of rewriting involved, or alterations of other kinds, then the story is likely a faulty one and the wisest strategy is to choose another story rather than disfigure the present one.

Having said so much by way of warning about what not to do, it must be said, too, that adapters are free to do as they please with a text, so long as their conscience will accept the aesthetic responsibility for the results.

In choosing a story for Chamber Theatre, the beginning director is apt to lean too heavily toward works with a lot of dialogue and action. Because of prior experience with these elements on the stage either as a spectator or director of conventional drama, he or she is comfortable with stories that feature these elements. There are stories, fine stories, in which the narration serves as little more than stage directions. Hemingway's "The Killers" is such a story; except for one brief reference to the interior condition of Nick Adams, there is nothing in the point of view which would be sacrificed by transferring the dialogue, action, and setting to the screen or the stage. If such stories are to be staged, they are best served by presenting them in conventional dramatic form.

Chamber Theatre is interested in presenting stories that depend for their value on the point of view expressed in the narration. It shares with conventional drama an interest in character and action, but the essence of its technique is in its concern for the narrative point of view. Since this must often be gleaned from the language of the descriptions and summaries, from the bone of the reports of the interior life of the characters, and from the general diction of the narration, it would be wise to choose stories that are rich in these features.

If it is necessary to cut the original text, be careful not to cut the climax or the key moment, or eliminate significant symbols, or so disproportion the movement of events that there is insufficient preparation for important actions. In brief, try not to distort the shape of the story in the process of abbreviating it. In a great, long novel, it may be necessary to make a major decision at the outset. It is impossible, for instance, to squeeze *Don Quixote, Moby-Dick,* or *Anna Karenina* onto the stage by cutting sentences and phrases here and there throughout the text. You might, therefore, decide to do Part One of *Don Quixote,* whose sanguine ending rounds off a unit complete in itself. You have, by that decision, reduced the text from 700 pages to 375, a major cut, to say the least. In *Moby-Dick,* you may find it profitable to stage only the three fateful days of Ahab's pursuit of the white whale that conclude this major work. In *Anna Karenina,* you may decide to eliminate Levin's story in order that Anna's might be more fully represented.

There are two kinds of cuts that should be made, generally speaking. The "he said's" and "she said's" should be cut because the presence of the actor and actress on stage engaging in dialogue make it perfectly plain who is speaking. The novelist is forced to use these phrases because it is the only way he or she has of indicating who is speaking. Sometimes even the printed text grows impatient with these clumsy tags and eliminates them once the direction of the dialogue has been established and the characters suffiently delineated. Some exceptions must be noted, however. These, like Eudora Welty's "Why I Live at the P.O.," have narrators who are circumstantial storytellers, given to a rhythmic identification of the speakers with "I says" and "She says." It would be a violation of style to cut such speech identifiers.

The other kind of cut that can be safely urged is the kind that eliminates brief narrative descriptions of action that the actors can perform quite satisfactorily. "He stood up, and turning to Madame A. said politely . . ." The actor can be trusted to stand up and turn to the actress playing Madame A. and to speak to her politely. Lest the generalization about cutting such descriptions be abused, it must be said that there are circumstances where it might be better to let the narrator or the character himself speak the words quoted above. Suppose that the character who is performing this action is concealing some irritation which inevitably colors his surface politeness. If the character or narrator prefaces his actual speech with these words, we can hear in the tone of voice the frozen calm, the icy composure, with which the character presumably addresses Madame A. In other words, the description can be used, not simply to identify the gross action, but to allow the tone of voice to express the emotional condition which is otherwise only inferred.

The director might well hestitate to cut those descriptions of action which include an attitude or comment on the part of the narrator. In Saki's "The Open Window" it might be asking too much of the actress playing Mrs. Sappleton to suggest in a single word what the narrator describes—" 'No?' said Mrs. Sappleton, in a voice which only replaced a yawn at the last minute." And it would certainly be asking too much of the actress playing Mrs. Stoner in "The Valiant Woman" to satisfy the narrator's description of her action in this passage:

> She swept up the cards and began to shuffle with the abandoned virtuosity of an old river boat gambler, standing them on end, fanning them out, whirling them through her fingers, dancing them halfway up her arms, cracking the whip over them. At last they lay before him tamed into a neat deck.[10]

The narrator's description here is an exaggeration of what Mrs. Stoner is actually doing and the description says more about the way Father Furman, her partner in the card game, *feels* about Mrs. Stoner than about the way she shuffles cards in any objective sense. There is, finally, no rule about cutting a novel or short story that can be applied without judicious review. Be prepared to reconsider your cutting during the staging of the story, for what may have seemed advisable in theory turns out to be inadvisable in practice.

In conclusion let me repeat: the adapter must be prepared to accept the aesthetic responsibility for any alterations or interpretations of the text, but certainly not in a fainthearted or apologetic manner. A thorough knowledge of the structure of the story will enable the adapter to make any necessary excisions with the authority and skill of a surgeon.

---

[10]Powers, "The Valiant Woman," p. 402.

8

SAMPLE SCRIPTS

If the critic is to avoid disfiguring literature in the process of atomizing it, he or she must possess, in addition to technical facility, intellectual grace—finesse. If the adapter would then restore life to the "etherized patient" so that the audience may appreciate the organic nature of the work, he or she must exercise creative intuition. At the risk of displaying a certain intellectual awkwardness and a more than occasional lapse of creative intuition, we shall attempt to provide some working samples of how the transition from the printed text to the fully realized story on the stage can be made. The scripts take the form of suggestions rather than prescriptions.

The stories are sufficiently complex to excite the imagination, but not so complex as to discourage a director's maiden effort in Chamber Theatre. They represent a range of problems: subjective and objective narrators, third-person and first-person narrators, cinematic techniques, direct and indirect discourse, etc. That the stories are all modern does not imply any prejudice against the literature of the past. While it is probably true that of all narrative forms the short story has enjoyed the richest development during the twentieth century nevertheless, it must be urged that all narrative literature from Homer to the latest bestseller is potential material for Chamber Theatre.

"IMPULSE"

Conrad Aiken's short story, "Impulse,"[1] concerns a young man who obeys an impulse to steal a trifle from a drugstore counter and is caught by a store detective. The pathos of the story derives, in part, from Michael Lowes' failure to realize that his is not an impulsive nature. We learn in subtle ways that he is more disposed to be calculating and scheming; we are not surprised to find that his impulsive act has failed. Since the story deals with the tension between two aspects of Michael Lowes' character, Aiken creates a narrator who is outside the story, who is objective and unprejudiced. But, since Michael's experience is essentially internal, the narrator must be privy to what goes on inside Michael, he must be omniscient.

The opening paragraph of "Impulse" tells us that

> Michael Lowes hummed as he shaved, amused by the face he saw—the pallid, asymmetrical face with the right eye so much higher than the left, and its eyebrow so peculiarly arched, like a "v" turned upside down. Perhaps this day wouldn't be as bad as the last. In fact, he knew it wouldn't be, and that was why he hummed. This was the bi-weekly day of escape, when he would stay out for the evening, and play bridge with Hurwitz, Bryant, and Smith. Should he tell Dora at the breakfast table? No, better not. Particularly in view of last night's row about unpaid bills. And there would be more of them, probably, beside his plate. The rent. The coal. The doctor who had attended to the children. Jeez, what a life. Maybe it was time to do a new jump. And Dora was beginning to get restless again—[2]

The first phrase, "Michael Lowes hummed as he shaved," is an objective observation available to anyone who might be privileged to share the bathroom with Michael. The second phrase, "amused by the face he saw," seems to be an observation no less objective than that contained in the first phrase, inasmuch as Michael probably smiled and indicated in an objective manner that it was his face that caused him to smile. Yet it must be understood that the narrator has reported only his interpretation of what he apparently observed. He has not given the objective evidence upon which his subjective judgments were based. Had the narrator said, "and smiled as he peered at his face in the mirror," the observation would have been clearly objective and the reader would have had to supply the interpretation that Michael was amused by his own face. Such interpretations are conventional and follow so readily from the objective evidence that the reader often fails to appreciate their subjective character.

Since human beings are denied the gift of omniscience, they facilitate their social intercourse by lending objective validity to hasty, subjective interpretations. Authors' narrators who have the gift of omniscience must exercise it with care in order to avoid straining the reading public's willingness to suspend its disbelief. Aiken's narrator skillfully leads the reader from Lowes' objective exterior to his intuited interior without any distressingly abrupt transitions.

Next, the narrator describes the face which amuses Michael. That it is Michael's own face which amuses him has to be assumed since it is never clearly identified as his. In fact, the narrator deliberately separates the face from Michael by referring to "*its* eyebrow." Such objectification of the face leads to another assumption: there must be a mirror, for that's the conventional way to see one's own face objectively. The mirror is easily assumed because Michael is shaving; since Aiken wrote the story before the advent of the electric razor, it is more than likely that Michael is shaving before a mirror.

The objective description of the face is subtly subjectified by the use of a simile, "like a 'v' turned upside down." Simile and metaphor by their nature suggest subjective interpretations. In this case, the emotional tone of the simile is not striking and, therefore, no sharp sense of Michael's inner state is conveyed.

Since the sentence, "Perhaps this day wouldn't be as bad as the last," is printed without quotation marks enclosing it, the reader assumes that the narrator is the speaker. But inasmuch as the narrator is omniscient, the conditional nature of "perhaps" can only be understood as relating to Michael's thoughts. It would seem that the narrator is speaking as though Michael's thoughts were being expressed directly. The narrator's use of "bad" to describe the day sounds less like his own characteristically formal speech and more like Michael's colloquial speech.

There is more than a hint of irony when the reader later discovers that "this day" is disastrous for Michael in a way that the "last" could not have been. The irony is emphasized in the next phrase, "In fact he knew it wouldn't be," because Michael's intuition is not to be trusted and, if one's intuition is not reliable, one had better not act impulsively.

The narrator began by giving us information which can be verified objectively—"Michael Lowes hummed"; now the reader learns from the narrator what Michael "knew" and the point of view becomes subjective.

When the narrator says, "Should he tell Dora . . .?" the interrogative structure of the statement suggests that the question originates in Michael and the reader begins to sense that it may be Michael himself speaking, though still through the intercession of the narrator. However, in the next statement, "No, better not," there is a reply to the question Michael has apparently proposed to himself. The narrator is still speaking, since there are still no quotation marks, but the reader continues to sense the tone of voice and inner presence of Michael.

Notice that Michael's reply to himself, "No, better not," is elliptical and informal. The manner of speaking here is less that of a third-person omniscient narrator outside the story than of a character inside the story speaking informally in the first person. The elliptical informality is suggested in the two sentences, "The rent. The coal." Finally, the narrator's informality and colloquial speech become unmistakable in "Jeez, what a life." The diction, the syntax, and the grammar all conspire to make us feel that we are listening not to the narrator but to Michael himself, despite the fact that the author has made it clear by his punctuation that the narrator and not Michael is responsible for the speech. The impression that Michael is now speaking persists to the end of the paragraph with another conditional word, "Maybe," and more colloquial speech, "do a new jump," and the punctuation at the end of the paragraph which suggests an informal interruption of Michael's free association.

The function of the narrator in "Impulse" is to lead us to an understanding of Michael from the inside. Since the omniscient point of view is both convenient and efficient, an author is tempted to employ it as a narrative device, but since it is a gift generally denied to human beings, it is a storytelling technique that must be used cautiously. Conrad Aiken very skillfully leads the reader from simple objective observations at the beginning of the story, and clearly omniscient statements by the narrator, to a condition of ambiguity when the reader recognizes the voice of Michael in the narrator's voice. In short, what Aiken has done is to insure objective reliability in reporting the inner life of Michael by using an omniscient narrator outside the story, yet moderating the narrator's omniscience by creating the illusion that the reader is hearing the authentic voice of Michael himself. The reader has been introduced subtly into the theatre of Lowes' psyche and there allowed to hear the inner voice of Michael uninterrupted by the narrator.

How can these narrative effects be expressed on the stage? One actor, playing Michael, hums, shaves, and observes his face in the mirror, while a second actor, playing the narrator, reports Michael's behavior to the audience. If this staging seems awkwardly redundant in that one actor pantomimes what another describes verbally, consider the burden placed on the actor who plays Michael of having to convey accurately the impression that he is amused by his own eyebrow which looks to him like a "v" turned upside down. In a conventional drama the problem would be solved by introducing a second character to whom Michael would explain that he was amused by his eyebrow which looks like a "v" turned upside down. But there is no greater economy in the conventional treatment, for it would take as many actors and as many words, and it is no more reasonable, perhaps, that Michael would be sharing the bathroom with a friend than that he should be sharing it with a narrator.

Another staging of the scene suggests itself: suppose that Michael confronts the narrator vis-à-vis and uses the latter's face as a mirror or shaving glass in which he sees his eyebrow. The physical relationship of Michael to the narrator would, in this case, accomplish several things: (1) it would put the narrator in an ideal position to observe closely the features of Michael's face; (2) it would suggest that the narrator's face is similar to, though not identical with, Michael's face simply because it is a mirror image; (3) the mirror image may appear somewhat different from Michael's inner vision of himself and this may well be the source of his amusement; (4) on the other hand, the physical resemblance of an object to its reflection might suggest to the audience that the narrator is in some way identified with Michael's inner life; and (5) any obvious difference between the narrator's appearance and Michael's would allow the audience to accept the possibility that the narrator speaks for that part of Michael which would be spontaneous and impulsive were it not for the other self (the one that is shaving, humming, and being amused) which is cautious, calculating, and shrewd. Perhaps it is these two aspects of his complex character that enter into a dialogue when the narrator says, "Should he tell Dora at the breakfast table?" and he is answered by the Michael who is cautious, "No, better not."

The director may decide to stage a cinematic interpretation of the scene. He may decide that the effectiveness of the scene depends on the audience seeing the full-face expressions of both the narrator and Michael. On the screen the audience would see first a full-face shot of Michael and then a full-face shot of his reflection in the mirror. The shots would alternate as the scene developed. To achieve this cinematic effect on the stage, the director will position both actors fullface toward the audience. Aside from the advantage of seeing the two images at once, this staging puts the audience physically in the position of the shaving glass and, at the same time, allows it to be in the position of Michael himself. The audience feels a dual responsibility in its reactions to man and mirror.

It is important to remember that Aiken's narrator speaks the entire paragraph while Michael shaves and hums. But it is also important to realize that as the diction and syntax of the narrator's speech change to create the impression that we are listening to Michael directly, we are experiencing a kind of ventriloquism. First we see Michael shaving and humming and we hear the narrator speaking; then we begin to have the illusion that we are hearing Michael himself speak. If one stages the scene so that Michael actually speaks the lines that most suit his tongue, then it would be advisable to let the narrator take up Michael's humming as though they had exchanged roles. If the narrator is allowed to represent an aspect of Michael which is in conflict with another aspect of his character then perhaps the narrator can change the tune which Michael has been humming.

Rather than risk confusing the director with further variations on the staging of "Impulse," let us consider in detail one particular organization of the scene for Chamber Theatre:

(Michael Lowes and the narrator are facing each other down stage center. Michael is humming a gay tune while he pantomimes shaving; he is looking directly into the face of the narrator as though it were a mirror.)

NAR: *(Holds his position steady so as not to disturb his function as mirror.)*
Michael Lowes hummed as he shaved.
(Michael interrupts his shaving and hums for a moment as he contemplates his face; laughs gently.)

NAR: Amused by the face he saw—the pallid, asymmetrical face, with the right eye so much higher than the left, and its eyebrow so peculiarly arched . . .
(Michael laughs again)

MIC: like a "v" turned upside down.
(Michael stops shaving and looks at mirror face of narrator—his razor suspended)

MIC: Perhaps this day wouldn't be as bad as the last.
(Michael resumes humming and recommences shaving)

NAR: In fact he knew it wouldn't be,
(Michael freezes; narrator turns his face to the audience)

NAR: and that was why he hummed.
(Michael resumes action, looking down into the basin while he rinses his razor; narrator continues to address the audience)

NAR: This was the bi-weekly day of escape, when he would stay out for the evening, and play bridge with Hurwitz, Bryant, and Smith.
(Michael looks into the mirror again as the narrator resumes his mirror position)

MIC: Should he tell Dora at the breakfast table?
(narrator and Michael in unison shake their heads slightly)

NAR: No, better not.
(Michael resumes shaving—humming a less lively tune)

NAR: Particularly in view of last night's row about unpaid bills. And there would be more of them, probably, beside his plate.

MIC: The rent. The coal.

NAR: The doctor who had attended the children.

MIC: Jeez, what a life. Maybe it was time to do a new jump.

NAR: And Dora was beginning to get restless again—

An examination of the second paragraph of "Impulse" shows a shift in the point of view. The staging of the first paragraph has hinted at the change we find in the Michael-narrator relationship to the audience in the second paragraph:

> But he hummed, thinking of the bridge game. Not that he liked Hurwitz, or Bryant, or Smith—cheap fellows, really—more pick-up acquaintances. But what could you do about making friends, when you were always hopping about from one place to another, looking for a living, and fate always against you! They were all right enough. Good enough for a little escape, a little party—and Hurwitz always provided good alcohol. Dinner at the Greek's, and then to Smith's room—yes. He would wait until late in the afternoon, and then telelphone to Dora as if it had all come up suddenly. Hello, Dora—is that you, old girl? Yes, this is Michael—Smith has asked me to drop in for a hand of bridge—you know—so I'll just have a little snack in town. Home by the last car as usual. Yes . . . Gooo-bye. . . .[3]

The opening phrase of this paragraph suggests that Michael has been humming all during the first paragraph except perhaps when his thoughts turn to "Jeez, what a life." Now, when his thoughts are on the bridge game, his spirits revive and he recommences humming. Again, there is an intrusion of colloquial diction into the narration, phrases like "cheap fellows" and "pick-up acquaintances." However, with the introduction of the second-person pronoun, the generalized "you," into the narration, the relationship of the narrator and of Michael to the audience becomes more direct. In the first paragraph the narrator was allowed to address the audience in order to make certain explanatory remarks. In the second paragraph, however, the generalized "you" suggests that Michael, the narrator, and the audience are all included; hence the narrator would very likely address his generalization to Michael *and* to the audience.

If the presence of the exclamation point after the phrase, "always against you!" should indicate to the director that the emotional level is too high for the impersonal third-person narrator, then he will probably assign the speech to Michael, who will address both the narrator and the audience.

[3]*Ibid.*, p. 15.

Beginning with "Hello, Dora—is that you, old girl?" to the end of the paragraph, it is clearly Michael speaking as though he were in the act of phoning his wife. The present tense and the first-person pronouns "me" and "I" are employed to strengthen our impression that Michael, and not the narrator, is speaking. Yet Aiken has given the speech to the narrator—why?—clearly to maintain the narrator's control of the story. The audience is not distressed by what seems at first to be a violation of the point of view because they realize that the phone conversation between Michael and Dora is, at this moment, simply a projection in time into the afternoon when Michael will actually make the call. They understand that the present speech is but an internal rehearsal of the afternoon call.

The second paragraph, like the first, ends with suspension points in order to suggest an informal, arbitrary truncation of Michael's thoughts. At this point the narrator seems to be largely absorbed into Michael's character.

The paragraph might be staged in this fashion:

(Michael hums a lively tune now; puts final touches on his shaving)

NAR: But he hummed, thinking of the bridge game.
　　(narrator turns to audience while Michael rinses razor)

NAR: Not that he liked Hurwitz, or Bryant, or Smith—

MIC: *(rinses face)* Cheap fellows, really—mere pick-up acquaintances.
　　(Michael reaches for towel which narrator hands him from the back of a chair which also contains Michael's shirt, tie, and jacket. Michael addresses audience as he dries his face and hands)

MIC: But what could you do about making friends, when you were always hopping about from one place to another, looking for a living, and fate always against you!
　　(hands towel back to narrator who gives him his shirt)

MIC: They were all right enough. *(puts on shirt)* Good enough for a little escape, a little party—and Hurwitz always provided good alcohol. Dinner at the Greek's, and then to Smith's room—yes.
　　(narrator hands Michael his tie)

NAR: He would wait until late in the afternoon, and then telephone to Dora as if it had all come up suddenly.
　　(Michael looks into narrator's face as the mirror to adjust his tie)

MIC: Hello, Dora—is that you, old girl? Yes, this is Michael—Smith has asked me to drop in for a hand of bridge—you know—
　　(narrator hands Michael his jacket which he puts on)

MIC: So I'll just have a little snack in town. Home by the last car as usual. Yes . . . Gooo-bye. . . .
　　(dim out)

"THE THIRD PRIZE"

A. E. Coppard has created an "objective" narrator who tells the story of "The Third Prize"[4] in the third person. Ordinarily such a narrator would be self-effacing, content to observe and report the action of the characters without comment. But in this story Coppard has allowed his narrator to express his own personality with some fullness and, indeed, to exercise considerable control over the story itself. The comic effect of the story depends to some extent on the contrast between the cultivated elevation of the narrator's style and the colloquial idiom of the major characters, who are plebs.

The setting of the story is a small provincial town about fifty miles from London and the occasion is a bank holiday, celebrated, in part, by a series of foot races which are entered by Naboth Bird, a mechanic by trade, and George Robins, a clerk. Their female companions are Minnie and Margery who "differ as much in character and temperament as Boadicea and Mrs. Hemans."[5]

The character of the third-person narrator must, of course, be inferred entirely from his spoken style. The actor who plays this role must see to it that his appearance and actions are consistent with the narrator's speech. Such portraits depend to a remarkable extent upon social stereotypes for their basic characterization of the objective narrator. Among students who study this story there is a strong consensus that either Clifton Webb or David Niven would be ideal for the role of the narrator in any movie version of "The Third Prize." The students evidently hear a vocal quality in the narrator's speech and see a manner of behavior in his words that consistently suggests a prototype in Webb and Niven.

The reader discovers in the opening paragraphs of Coppard's story that the principal features of the small provincial town are a military garrison and a dockyard. The narrator says:

> On their [Bird's and Robin's] arrival they found almost the entire populace wending to the carnival of games in a long stream of soldiers, sailors, and quite ordinary people, harried by pertinacious and vociferous little boys who yelled: "Program?"[6]

The reference to the people of the town as "populace" suggests a slightly

[4]A. E. Coppard, "The Third Prize," in *Short Story Masterpieces*, p. 115-123.
[5]*Ibid.*, p. 115.
[6]*Ibid.*, p. 115.

elevated tone; "wending" is sufficiently poetic or archaic to seem inappropriate to a crowd of soldiers, sailors, and ordinary people in a small garrison and dockyard town of the "late nineties." Calling the local footraces a "carnival of games" gives them a classical dignity reminiscent of the Olympic games. The use of the intensifier, "quite," in referring to the ordinary people plus the latinated description of the little boys as "pertinacious" and "vociferous" reveal a taint of snobbery in the narrator.

When the narrator speaks of the "two jolly girls, Margery and Minnie, [who] by some pleasant alchemy soon attached themselves to our two runners,"[7] he is talking over their heads. He does not adjust his expressions to the level of their understanding; they would not know what he meant by "alchemy" nor would they appreciate his likening them to Boadicea and Mrs. Hemans. The narrator's tone of superiority is complicated by his momentary condescension when he refers to Naboth and George as "our two runners." The possessive pronoun is slightly presumptuous and reminds us of the way that nineteenth-century novelists expressed their proprietary relationship as "our hero."

Despite the narrator's apparent superiority to the characters in his story he takes an intense interest in their conversations and seems to enjoy adopting their diction. Here is a section of the story that reports the opening gambit in the relationship between Margery and George:

> "From London you come!" exclaimed George. "How'd you get here?"
> The young lady crisply testified that she came in a train—did the fathead think she had swum? They were jolly glad when they got here, too and all. Carriage full, and ructions all the way.
> "Ructions! What ructions?"
> "Boozy men! Half of 'em trying to cuddle you."
> Mr. Robins intimated that he could well understand such desires. Miss Margery retorted that then he was understanding much more than was good for him. Mr. Robins thought not, he hoped not. Miss Margery indicated that he could hope for much more than he was likely to get. Mr. Robins replied that, he would do that, and then double it. And he asserted, with all respect, that had he but happily been in that train he too might have, etc. and so on. Whereupon Miss Margery snapped, Would he? and Mr. Robins felt bound to say Sure!
> "Would you—well, I'll tell you what I did to one of them." And she told him. It was quite unpleasant.[8]

Notice that George is allowed in the opening line of this passage to

[7]*Ibid*., p. 115.
[8]*Ibid*., p. 116.

exclaim and put a question to Margery in his own voice, but immediately the narrator steps in and summarizes Margery's reply. The narrator maintains his elevated diction in those words that serve as signs of indirect discourse: "testified," "intimated," "retorted," "indicated," and "asserted." But he also slips into the diction of her speech: "fathead," "jolly glad," "too and all," and "ructions."

It must be emphasized that though "ructions" is Margery's word, it is from the narrator that the reader learns the expression. When George responds in his own voice and says, "Ructions! What ructions?" he is, of course, responding to Margery's speech as a primary source and to the narrator's speech as a secondary source of the word, "ructions." The fact that there are no narrative "tags" to identify George as the speaker or Margery as the one who replies to him with "Boozy men! Half of 'em trying to cuddle you," creates the impression that George responds directly to the narrator even as Margery responds directly to George. The ultimate effect of George's response to the narrator and Margery's response to George is to include the narrator actively in their conversation. Active inclusion of the narrator together with his acceptance of their diction establishes his sympathetic interest.

At the risk of being too atomistic it should be noted that at the end of the second paragraph of indirect discourse the narrator puts Margery's question in the third person, "Would he?" whereas, in direct discourse, Margery would have used the second person, "Would you?" The change in person clearly places the ultimate responsibility for the speech on the narrator. It is equally true, but less apparent, that the narrator is responsible for Mr. Robins' reply when the narrator says, "Mr. Robins felt bound to say Sure!" Mr. Robins' word of reply, "Sure!" has the capitalization and the exclamation mark to establish the remark as his, but in the printed text there are no quotation marks embracing the word and so we must conclude that though George said the word, the reader must hear it echoed in the voice of the narrator. When Margery responds directly to the narrator's proxy statement of "Sure!" with a speech employing the second person, "Would you . . ." it seems as though Margery is surely responding more directly to the narrator than to George.

The general effect of this passage in "The Third Prize" is to bring the narrator into an intimate relation with the characters. The Chamber Theatre staging of the passage should foster that effect. The narrator should retain his cultured diction but he should slip into the dialect and speech manner of George and Margery when he uses their diction in the indirect discourse.

The final statement in the passage quoted above is clearly an expression of the narrator's character. Margery has willingly confessed to George what she did to one of the men on the train. The narrator, however, is unwilling to share with the reader what she said. This unwillingness confirms his control over what the reader is to learn. His reason for withholding information may be entirely personal; he may simply find Margery's confession "quite unpleasant." On the other hand, his reticence about repeating what Margery told George may signal his respect for the delicate sensibilities of the reader. In any case, the decision to remain silent is an expression of the narrator's character.

The following arrangement of the passage under discussion is but one interpretation of the relationship of the narrator to the characters and to the action. This particular view of the scene suggests that the narrator has a "gossipy" interest in what is going on and that he reports his story in much the same fashion as the unsophisticated storyteller who liberally sprinkles his/her narrative with "he said's" and "she said's." The fact that Coppard's narrator is as liberal in his use of "intimated," "retorted," "indicated," etc. as another might be with the more conventional "he said's" and "she said's" makes for comic incongruity and says something rather specific about the character of the narrator.

It should be understood that George and Margery are talking steadily while the narrator repeats their conversation. They are saying in the first person what the narrator reports in the third person. The speeches must be so orchestrated and the volume so controlled that the audience is not left in the dark as to what they are saying or what the narrator is saying. However, if a certain amount of confusion is created, the effect is not without its justification because there are a lot of people about on the fair grounds and the atmosphere is one of general excitement:

(George and Margery are downstage center facing each other with enough space between them to allow for necessary observation and appraisal. George has set his cap back slightly on his head; Margery has set her purse in motion. The narrator, well-dressed with cane and gloves, stands between them and slightly upstage of them)

GEO: From London you come! How'd you get here?

NAR: *(looking at Margery)* The young lady crisply testified.

MAR: I came in a train, fathead.

NAR: She came in a train.

MAR: Do you think I swum?

NAR: Did the fathead think she had swum? *(looking at George)*

MAR: We were jolly glad when we got here, too and all.

NAR: They were jolly glad when they got here, too and all.

MAR: Carriage full, and ructions all the way.

NAR: *(does not repeat "Carriage full")* Ructions all the way.

GEO: Ructions! What ructions?

MAR: Boozy men! Half of 'em trying to cuddle you.

(During the following speech by the narrator, George and Margery impro-
vise their banter so that his speech and theirs are simultaneous or perhaps
interwoven. The narrator glances from George to Margery and from
Margery to George as their speeches alternate, creating the effect of watch-
ing a tennis match)

NAR: Mr. Robins intimated that he could well understand such desires.
Miss Margery retorted that then he was understanding much more
than was good for him. Mr. Robins thought not, he hoped not. Miss
Margery indicated that he could hope for much more than he was
likely to get. Mr. Robins replied that, he would do that, and double
it. And he asserted with all respect that had he but happily been in
that train he too might have, etc., and so on. Whereupon Miss
Margery snapped, would he? And Mr. Robins felt bound to say
Sure!

MAR: Would you—well, I'll tell you what I did to one of them.

NAR: And she told him. It was quite unpleasant.

Other arrangements of the scene are possible. It might, for instance, seem advisable to let the narrator speak that part of the indirect
discourse that introduces the summaries of the character's direct speech.
Let the narrator say, "The young lady crisply testified that . . ." and let
Margery say, "she came in a train—did the fathead think she had
swum?"

When the character speaks his own section of the indirect discourse
there is sometimes a discrepancy between his own native diction and that
of the indirect discourse. For example, if the narrator were to say, "And
he [George] asseted, with all respect, that . . ." and then George, himself, were to complete the statement "had he but happily been in that
train he might have . . ." we would notice the elevation in George's diction. This "unnaturalness" need not prevent the use of it in Chamber
Theatre productions. It is, perhaps, no more peculiar to hear George
speak in an elevated tone than to hear the narrator speak in a more
vulgar tone when reporting conversations in indirect discourse. The
effect is finally one of alienation. To hear unaccustomed speech from
either the narrator or the character is to alert the listener to the fact that
the author and the actors are not far apart and that the illusion of social
reality is being modified in such a way as to make it clear that what is
going on is a "demonstration" of relationships and not simply the expo-
sure of social reality itself. When the narrator and the characters share
the incongruities of diction a comic tone is assured, and a sympathetic
rapport is established by the mutual exchange of languages. These ben-
efits are subtle and indirectly achieved, but nonetheless valuable.

"THE BRIDE COMES TO YELLOW SKY"

There is a special exhilaration experienced by visitors to a Hollywood sound stage where a scene is being shot. There is a thrill in being allowed to see *how* the illusion is created; the pleasure given by the illusion offered on the screen seems to be augmented by the visitor's initiation into the craft of film making. The same special delight is available to audiences who would like to see a little more particularly how a story is put together. The use of film techniques in staging a story may create for an audience the impression that they are seeing a story made as well as seeing the story itself. A text that lends itself admirably to such a treatment is Stephen Crane's short story, "The Bride Comes to Yellow Sky."[9] The occasional pockets of violence and male aggression that once characterized the Wild West are apt now to be pathetic and shabby; what in a shoot-out was once romantic is now lackluster because it is chiefly the sport of drunkards.

The tone of frontier extravagance, still traditional in Texas and still amusing to the remainder of the country is mocked slightly in the opening paragraph of the story:

> The great Pullman was whirling onward with such dignity of motion that a glance from the window seemed simply to prove that the plains of Texas were pouring eastward. Vast flats of green grass, dull-hued spaces of mesquit and cactus, little groups of frame houses, woods of light and tender trees, all were sweeping into the east, sweeping over the horizon, a precipice.[10]

The final metaphor, "sweeping over the horizon, a precipice," overstates the poetic condition, especially when one realizes that the great stretches of grass, mesquit, cactus, and woods are being surveyed from the plush comfort of "the great Pullman" which is carrying Jack Potter, the marshall of Yellow Sky, home with his new bride from "San Anton." A marshall with a wife is contrary to the tradition of the Old West and Potter was aware that in marrying this woman "he had committed an extraordinary crime." His submission to the shackles of domesticity left only one standard bearer of the frontier code—Scratchy Wilson, "the last one of the old gang that used to hang out along the river here." When Potter arrives in Yellow Sky with his new bride he runs into Scratchy who is on a drunken spree and shooting up the town:

[9]Stephen Crane, "The Bride Comes to Yellow Sky," *Short Story Masterpieces*, pp. 124-136. Reprinted by permission of the University Press of Virginia.
[10]*Ibid.*, p. 124.

The two men faced each other at a distance of three paces. He of the revolver smiled with a new and quiet ferocity. "Tried to sneak up on me!" His eyes grew more baleful. As Potter made a slight movement, the man thrust his revolver venomously forward. "No; don't do it, Jack Potter. Don't you move a finger toward a gun just yet. Don't you move an eyelash. . . ."

Potter looked at his enemy. "I ain't got a gun on me, Scratchy," he said. "Honest, I ain't. . . . You'll have to do all the shootin' yourself."

His enemy's face went livid. He stepped forward, and lashed his weapon to and fro before Potter's chest. "Don't tell me you ain't got no gun on you, you whelp. Don't tell me no lie like that. . . . Don't take me for no kid." His eyes blazed with light, and his throat worked like a pump.

"I tell you I ain't got a gun, and I ain't. If you're goin' to shoot me up, you better begin now; you'll never get a chance like this again."

So much enforced reasoning had told on Wilson's rage; he was calmer. "If you ain't got a gun, why ain't you got a gun?" he sneered. "Been to Sunday-school?"

"I ain't got a gun because I've just come from San Anton' with my wife. I'm married," said Potter.

"Married!" said Scratchy, not at all comprehending.

"Yes, married. I'm married," said Potter distinctly.[11]

The point of view of the narrator must be clearly defined in any staging of a Chamber Theatre production, but nowhere is definition more critical than when the narrator is acting as the camera and the film director. In the case of "The Bride Comes to Yellow Sky" the narration provides the tone of a cheap Western, full of cliches and overacting. Phrases like "His eyes blazed with light," "His enemy's face went livid," and "his throat worked like a pump" suggest that the narrator is supercharging the characters with emotions that will lend importance to a very hackneyed situation. The dialogue is repetitious and flat, the characters are two dimensional, the action is essentially comic. This tone is deliberately cultivated by the style Crane puts into the mouth of the narrator. The absurdities of the story are set against the nostalgia we all have for the genuine West. And there are hints of that West to be found in Crane's story; for example, Scratchy, though drunk, missed the target he set up on the saloon door by half an inch when he fired at it from the street. The townspeople respected Scratchy's marksmanship and called him "a wonder with a gun—a perfect wonder."

Since no actual cameras will be used in the shooting of this scene, it is necessary that the narrator/director employ some typical devices for

---

[11]*Ibid.,* p. 135.

suggesting the camera. He can wear a finder on a cord about his neck, which he looks through like a telescope to adjust the focus of the lens before shooting; he can put the tips of his thumbs together and spread his palms away from them to simulate the camera frame through which he looks to get an idea of what will be included in the frame when the shot is made. He can improvise speech to the technicians operating the camera, saying: "I want a real tight shot on the throat, I really want to see it pump—that's it (as the imagined camera moves closer and the director gives way to let it move in tight), real tight. O.K., now Scratchy, tighten the cords in your neck a little, that's it. O.K. we're ready." At this point, an actor playing the assistant director "slates" the scene and bangs the clapboard in front of Scratchy's face, saying: "Scene thirty-five, take one." The director says, "Camera," and the actor with the clapboard, speaking for the camera man says: "Rolling" (pause), "Speed" (pause), and the director says, "Action" and Scratchy stands with his neck cords tensed while the camera takes a tight shot of what the director now describes: "his throat worked like a pump" and we, the audience, see what the camera sees as the actor playing Scratchy swallows repeatedly to make his Adam's apple move up and down like a pump handle.

An important feature of the filming of this scene is that it is a series of full-face close-ups which are seen in the movie theatre as just that, full-face close-ups. In other words we see Scratchy on the screen, but we do not, at the same time, see Potter; then, in the next shot we see Potter facing us, while there is no sign of Scratchy. It is true that in the opening shot, the cameraman sees the two men facing each other in profile rather than facing us, but most of the subsequent shots that make up the scene show each of the characters facing the camera and not each other. To reproduce this effect on the stage, Scratchy and Potter, after they have faced each other on the opening shot, will face the audience as they stand side by side. To suggest alienation, only the actor who is being "shot" needs to be "in character" since he is the only one whom the camera sees. The other actor can drop out of character, smoke a cigarette, chat with the assistant director or the actress who is playing Potter's wife and has little to do in the full scene, then take his place and get into character when it is in his turn to be "shot."

The staging of Crane's story, as a film being shot in a studio, allows the audience to see it as a cheap "Western" containing characters that are remnants of a vanishing culture, who do that culture little honor. The tone of the story is more complex than this simplified staging suggests; nevertheless, there is value in treating it cinematically. Some suggestions have already been made about how the narrator/director handles the actors and controls the mechanics of shooting the scenes, but a closer, though not necessarily fuller, look at how the whole scene might be staged filmically is in order:

(The NARRATOR/DIRECTOR *places a chalk mark just left of stage center*—"Potter, this is your mark, and Scratchy, this is yours"—NAR/DIR *steps off three paces*—"O.K., Charlies, I want a wide shot here, but close; bring it up to about here"—*he marks a spot about six feet downstage of the two actors who have taken their positions on their marks and are facing each other*—"O.K., slate it, George"—George *slates the scene, then says,* "Quiet, please, Scene 28, Take one"—*claps the board,* NAR/DIR *steps back to give the camera full room*—"Camera"—George *says*—"Rolling" *(pause)* "Speed" *(pause)*—NAR/DIR "Action—'The two men faced each other at a distance of three paces'—Cut—Print it"—NAR/DIR *turns Scratchy ninety degrees to face the audience*—"Stay on your mark, I want to catch your smile full-face. Charlie, make this shot close and tight, I want to kill the background as much as possible, and feature the beard, the missing teeth, and all the crow's feet, you know?"—NAR/DIR *measures the distance with his finder or his two hands put up before his eyes like a framing device. Same procedure is followed as in scene 28. Potter is not included in the shot so he can relax and drop out of character. After the* NAR/DIR *says* "Action," *he speaks the line of narration that is being filmed with a kind of mock heroic tone and gesture, for certainly the style of the phrase* "He of the revolver" *referring to Scratchy, a pathetic, antediluvian, old drunk is a mockery. He says*—"He of the revolver smiled with a new and quiet ferocity")

SCR: Tried to sneak up on me! Tried to sneak up on me!

NAR/DIR: Cut! Print! That was good, it had the right quality of quiet intensity and j-u-s-t enough ferocity. *(He laughs and hugs Scratchy playfully)*

The remainder of the scene is played out in the same fashion with improvised directions for the camera work and the actor's interpretations, plus narration and dialogue. In order to speed up the movement of the scene, the camera directions and the slating can be abbreviated or eliminated. But don't let the scene move too fast—it is a formal scene with lots of intensity which can be made to pay off theatrically, if the tempo is retarded without reducing intensity. Remember that the director's intensity in controlling the shots contributes to the intensity of the scene between Scratchy and Potter.

"A COUNTRY LOVE STORY"

The recent preference for shooting films on location has popularized the use of hand-held cameras because they create a documentary effect. They are smaller and more flexible than the studio pedestal cameras and give the effect of on-the-spot coverage. In the hands of a narrator in a Chamber Theatre production, such a camera, because of its portability and flexibility, would speed up the action and allow it to run more continuously. The use of the hand-held camera in staging a scene from Jean Stafford's short story, "A Country Love Story,"[12] may demonstrate its effectiveness in directing the audience's attention to those critical details so necessary for understanding this elusive passage, which involves hallucinating, dreaming, and waking. A real camera is used but, of course, no film is actually shot.

In the passage preceding the one we shall study, May has suffered an hallucination in which she sees her lover. The staging of this passage would allow the audience to see the lover, too, dressed and acting exactly as May describes him, but the narrator would not film the hallucination; he would film only May—she is real and would show up on the film; the hallucinated lover, of course, would not. In the passage we are about to review, the narrator will film May and Daniel as the audience sees them in their corporeal reality; the lover and May in the dream will not be filmed. The filming of May and Daniel will resume after May wakens.

The passage commences with May, Daniel's wife, looking out her window one night to see "her lover sitting in the sleigh." Heretofore, she had only imagined him, but now, at this present moment, he is an hallucination because she says, "He was younger than she had imagined him to be." He is described in detail as to dress, complexion, hair, etc. He vanishes and only then is she able to sleep, and, not unexpectedly, she dreams of him:

> That night she slept a while. She lay near to Daniel, who was smiling in the moonlight. She could tell that the sleep she would have tonight would be as heavy as a coma, and she was aware of the moment she was overtaken.
>
> She was in a canoe in a meadow of water lilies and her lover was tranquilly taking the shell off a hard-boiled egg. "How intimate," he said, "to eat an egg with you." She was nervous lest the canoe tip over, but at the same time she was charmed by his wit and by the way he lightly touched her shoulder with the varnished paddle.
>
> "May? May? I love you, May."
>
> "Oh!" enchanted, she heard her voice replying. "Oh, I love you, too!"
>
> "The winter is over, May. You must forgive the hallucinations of a sick man."
>
> She woke to see Daniel's fair, pale head bending toward her. "He is old! He is ill!" she thought, but through her tears, to deceive him one last time, she cried, "Oh, thank God, Daniel!"
>
> He was feeling cold and wakeful and he asked her to make him a cup of tea; before she left the room, he kissed her hands and arms and said, "If I am ever sick again, don't leave me, May."[13]

[12]Jean Stafford, "A Country Love Story," in *Short Story Masterpieces*, pp. 440-454.
[13]*Ibid.*, pp. 451-453.

To simplify matters, we will assume that May and Daniel are sitting on a bench in stage center, facing the audience. May is sitting right of Daniel and the narrator, with his handheld camera, is down right of May:

(Daniel is already asleep and May is settling into sleep. The narrator is winding up his hand-held camera, preparing to take a shot of May.)

NAR: That night she slept a while. *(shoots for a few moments in silence, then moves up left toward Daniel saying, "She lay near to Daniel" goes down on one knee to get a shot of Daniel from below)* "who was smiling in the moonlight." *(narrator stops filming, rises and moves further left and then right, above the bench, circling back behind May as she says—)*

MAY: She could tell that the sleep she would have tonight would be as heavy as a coma, and she was aware of the moment she was overtaken.

(narrator moves into his original position down right—slowly, as he says—)

NAR: She was in a canoe in a meadow of water lilies and her lover . . . *(narrator sits cross-legged on the floor, a canoe's length from May)* was tranquilly taking the shell off a hard-boiled egg. "How intimate to eat an egg with you."

MAY: She was nervous lest the canoe tip over, but at the same time she was charmed by his wit and by the way he lightly touched her shoulder with the varnished paddle.

(Daniel, waking, touches her shoulder. Narrator and Daniel share the next speech with the narrator saying the first "May" alone, then joined by Daniel on the second "May." Then, while Daniel is saying the second "May," the narrator is saying, "I love you." The effect is that of a "round" or an echo. The speech can be repeated as often or with such variations as seem best to create a slightly unreal atmosphere for May. In a half sleep she addresses her speech to the narrator who is still sitting in the canoe.)

MAY: Oh!

NAR: Enchanted she heard her voice replying . . .

(May to narrator)

MAY: Oh, I love you, too!

DAN: The winter is over, May. You must forgive the hallucinations of a sick man.

(May wakens and turns slowly toward Daniel who puts his head slowly on her shoulder. The narrator rises and moves slowly left upstage of the bench. Narrator begins to film again.)

NAR: She woke to see Daniel's fair, pale head bending toward her.

(Narrator by now is behind Daniel upstage at the left end of the bench looking at May. And she is looking at the narrator, saying—)

MAY: He is old! He is ill!

(narrator is filming May)

NAR: She thought, but through her tears, to deceive him one last time, she cried . . .

MAY: Oh, thank God, Daniel.
(Narrator moves right slightly in order to film Daniel from upstage of the bench)

DAN: He was feeling cold and wakeful. *(very quietly, almost inaudibly, Daniel says—)*
I feel cold, May—would you make me a cup of tea? *(while the narrator says—)*

NAR: And he asked her to make him a cup of tea. *(May answers in the same quiet tone)* "Yes, of course, right away."
(May rises from the bench and moves slowly toward the door down left. The narrator follows her half way, filming her. When the narrator speaks she stops and turns back toward Daniel.)

NAR: Before she left the room . . .
(Having turned toward Daniel, May sees that he is holding out his arms to her in a pathetic, pleading gesture. She returns to Daniel. The narrator turns as she passes him, filming all the while)

NAR: He kissed her hands and arms.

DAN: If I am ever sick again, don't leave me, May.
(May slowly disengages herself and moves through the exit down left. The narrator follows her half way to the exit, filming as he moves. He continues to film May for a moment or two after she has left. He stops filming and winds his camera as Daniel settles back weakly into a half sleep.)

"WHY I LIVE AT THE P.O."

The problems of staging a story told in the first person are somewhat different from those we have met in our discussion of stories told by narrators in the third person. In third-person points of view the separation between what is told and what is shown is relatively clear. The position of the first-person narrator is somewhat more ambiguous, for this character appears as a vital physical presence to other characters in the story while enjoying the privilege of direct address to the reader or audience. There is a precedent for this practice in nineteenth-century melodramas when the "aside" was in common use. But with the development of realism in the theatre, any direct recognition of the audience was regarded as an aesthetic fault. However, by the middle of the twentieth century the theatre had become more congenial to the practice of directly addressing the audience and today it is far from uncommon. First-person narration in fiction has always been considered an address to the reader and Chamber Theatre is prepared to take advantage of that tradition in practice on the stage.

Authors sometimes find it necessary to tell a story from the point of view of a character quite other than their own. They create a character with a name and a personality distinct from their own and, in order that the reader may understand the character, an author will create the fictional world as it is refracted or distorted by the human bias of the first-person narrator. There is no sounder way to understand someone other than one's self than to see the world as he sees it.

Eudora Welty has created Sister, the first-person narrator of "Why I Live at the P.O.,"[14] so that the reader may see the world as a paranoiac sees it. Even though the characters in her story speak in direct discourse, the reader is not altogether satisfied that his dialogue is a faithful copy of the original, for what they say is subject to the prejudicial recall of Sister, the narrator. The story of her experiences with her family on that fateful Fourth of July is entirely recollected so that we cannot accept it with the same unqualified suspension as we would the testimony of a third-person narrator. We may, at first, be impressed with the circumstantiality of Sister's story since she seems to remember everything with remarkable concreteness and vividness. As the story progresses, however, doubts about its authenticity begin to arise; the reader begins to notice certain hyperbolic remarks: Papa-Daddy is "about a million years old," Mama "weighs two hundred pounds and has real tiny feet," and "Uncle Rondo had all the brains of the entire family."

The matter of physical setting is important in "Why I Live at the P.O." It is not until the end of the story that we learn that Sister's account is directed to someone in the "P.O." Sister has related the scenes of her life at home so vividly that the past seems to have more immediacy for her than does the "present," concluding scene in the Post Office. In a Chamber Theatre production of this work some peripheral area of the stage—downstage right, perhaps—must be reserved for the "P.O." while the central area of the stage serves for the recollected scenes. Though Sister protests that she is happy living at the "P.O.," the audience soon learns that the emotional center of her life is in the bosom of her family.

In the opening paragraph of the story Sister introduces her family to the listener. Then follows her recollections of the Fourth of July, the day her sister, Stella-Rondo, turned up unexpectedly at dinner time when the family was at table and Sister was busy in the kitchen preparing and serving the meal all by herself, since the Negro help had the day off. Area lighting would pick up Sister downstage right talking to the audience which she regards as the collective listener in the "P.O." she says, "I was getting along fine with Mama (a special light comes up on Mama sitting on a chair in the central area of the stage as though waiting to be served at dinner), Papa-Daddy (another special light comes up on

---

[14]Eudora Welty, "Why I Live at the P.O.," in *Short Story Masterpieces*, pp. 525-538. Reprinted by permission of Harcourt Brace Jovanovich, Inc.

Papa-Daddy in the same area laboriously tucking in his napkin with palsied hands), and Uncle Rondo (special light comes up on Uncle Rondo who is standing near Papa-Daddy, his back three-quarters to the audience and drinking a long slug of 'prescription' from a bottle) until my sister Stella-Rondo (light comes up on Stella-Rondo standing near Mama and wearing a big floppy-brimmed hat and holding a young child by the hand) just separated from her husband and came back home again."

This, then, is the physical relationship on the stage of the characters at the beginning of the following scene which is only thirteen lines further along in the story:

> So as soon as she got married and moved away from home the first thing she did was separate! from Mr. Whitaker! This photographer with the popeyes she said she trusted. Came home from one of those towns up in Illinois and to our complete surprise brought this child of two.
>
> Mama said she like to made her drop dead for a second. "Here you had this marvelous blond child and never so much as wrote your mother a word about it," says Mama. "I'm thoroughly ashamed of you." But of course she wasn't.
>
> Stella-Rondo just calmly takes off this *hat*, I wish you could see it. She says, "Why, Mama, Shirley-T.'s adopted, I can prove it."
>
> "How?" says Mama, but all I says was, "H'm!" There I was over the hot stove, trying to stretch two chickens over five people and a completely unexpected child into the bargain, without one moment's notice.
>
> "What do you mean—'H'm!'" says Stella-Rondo, and Mama says, "I heard that, Sister."
>
> I said that oh, I didn't mean a thing, only that whoever Shirley-T. was, she was the spit-image of Papa-Daddy if he'd cut off his beard, which of course he'd never do in the world. Papa-Daddy's Mama's papa and sulks.[15]

The script for a Chamber Theatre production of this passage might take the following form:

SIS: *(moves from the P.O. area down right to the kitchen area down left putting an apron on and turning up the sleeves of her blouse)*
So as soon as she got married and moved away from home the first thing she did was separate! From Mr. Whitaker! This photographer with the popeyes she said she trusted.
(Sister is in the kitchen area now and pantomimes the process of getting the food ready to serve)

[15]*Ibid.*, pp. 525-526.

Came home from one of those towns up in Illinois and to our complete surprise brought this child of two.
(lights now illuminate Mama, Stella, and child in a single area. Stella and the child move down to Mama; there is improvised dialogue of greeting between mother and daughter. Sister moves to the door of the kitchen to observe the reunion.)
Mama says she like to made her drop dead for a second.

MAM: Here you had this marvelous blonde child and never so much as wrote your mother a word about it.

SIS: Says Mama.

MAM: I'm thoroughly ashamed of you.

SIS: But of course she wasn't. Stella-Rondo just calmly takes off this *hat*, I wish you could see it.* She says . . .

STE: Why, Mama, Shirley-T.'s adopted, I can prove it.

MAM: How?

SIS: Says Mama, but all I says was, "H'm!" *(goes back into kitchen area)* There I was over a hot stove, trying to stretch two chickens over five people and a completely unexpected child into the bargain, without a moment's notice.
(Sister now appears in the dining room area with the first of her hot dishes which she places on the dining table)

STE: What do you mean—"H'm!"?

SIS: Says Stella-Rondo, and Mama says . . .

MAM: I heard that, Sister.

SIS: *(addresses audience as the collective listener in the P.O.—action in the dining area is frozen as in still life)*
I said that oh, I didn't mean a thing, only that whatever Shirley-T. was, she was the spit-image of Papa-Daddy if he'd cut off his beard, which of course he'd never do in the world. Papa-Daddy's Mama's papa and sulks.

---

*Certain specific effects follow from the presence of the phrase "I wish you could see it."

1. If Stella-Rondo is actually wearing a hat, then the audience can see for itself what it looks like, and Sister's remark seems unnecessary. However, this very duplication reminds the audience that it is the collective listener in the "P.O.," and that the hat, as part of the recollected event, is not available for inspection by the listener in the present. The audience is forced to regard itself as being simultaneously present in the virtual past and in the actual present.

2. If the phrase, "I wish you could see it," is cut and Stella-Rondo is allowed to remove her hat in silence there is dramatic emphasis placed upon the hat and Stella-Rondo's vanity—perhaps, in the way she removes it. In other words, the removal of the hat in silence might say something about Stella and the way Sister remembers her.

3. If Stella-Rondo does not actually wear a hat but simply removes an imaginary one, the audience may well agree with Sister that it beggars description and it is no wonder that Sister must need identify it simply as "*hat.*"

The decision to stop the stage action of the family during Sister's final speech in this passage stems from certain changes in the narrative technique that Miss Welty effects: (1) In the dialogue immediately preceding the final paragraph, Sister has used the historical present, "she says," and "Mama says." The use of this tense is customary with unsophisticated storytellers who instinctively recognize the importance of giving their listeners a sense of the immediacy of the events they are recounting. In this final paragraph, however, Sister shifts to the past tense, "I said that oh, I didn't mean a thing. . . ." The change of tenses suggests a shift in focus—in the present tense the emphasis is on the remembered event, whereas the past tense emphasizes the narrator's present relationship to the listener in the "P.O."; hence the action in the family scene is halted while Sister relates to the "P.O." listener.

(2) The action is stopped in order to make sure that the audience understands that what Mama and Stella-Rondo heard in the past—"Oh, I *don't* mean a thing"—is now what the "P.O." listener hears in the present as "oh, I *didn't* mean a thing." When the audience is to be made most aware of the past as immediate then the present tense and quotation marks are employed. But when the audience is to be made most aware of the present time in the "P.O." then the past tense is used and the quotation marks are removed.

In short, Eudora Welty has constructed Sister's story in such a way as to allow the reader or listener to have a simultaneous image of Sister as she appears in the "P.O." and as she appears in the remembered events that took place in the bosom of her family.

The Chamber Theatre arrangement of the text printed here tends to minimize the distinction between the two images of Sister by allowing one actress to play the part and to so generalize the "P.O." setting that it becomes absorbed into the home setting. The only acknowledgment of differences between what is said in the "P.O." and what is clearly remembered as having been said at home is that Sister addresses the audience as the collective auditor when she is speaking from the "P.O." and addresses the characters on stage when she is speaking in the remembered scenes. However, the director may prefer to make the structure of the story clearer to his audience by allowing two actresses to play the part of Sister—one in the "P.O." downstage right and one who performs in the remembered action. The audience would see both Sisters, one in the past and one in the present.

Should the director choose to use two actresses, then the "P.O." Sister would speak the first and last speeches of the section printed here. The "P.O." Sister might also say, "But of course she wasn't" which is clearly an aside to the listener by way of further elucidation of Sister's paranoiac conviction that Mama favors Stella-Rondo. Perhaps, too, both Sisters could share the last speech with the main focus on the "P.O." Sister saying: "I said that oh, I didn't mean a thing . . ." etc., while the

Sister in the family scene simultaneously says, "Oh, I don't mean a thing . . ." etc. Notice that the first Sister uses the form of indirect discourse and the past tense of the original text, while the Sister in the remembered action uses direct discourse and the present tense which is consistent with her previous speeches under the same conditions.

Simultaneity of setting ("P.O." and family home) and simultaneity of past and present are important features of the structure of "Why I Live at the P.O." A Chamber Theatre treatment of the story cannot ignore the problems that arise from the staging of that simultaneity. Nevertheless, much or little can be made of it according to the sensibilities and intentions of the director. For example, Miss Welty does not let the reader in on the fact that Sister is really speaking from the "P.O." until the story is almost finished, when the narrator changes the tense of her narration from past to present.

Keeping the reader ignorant of Sister's physical locus at the beginning of the story is aesthetically functional, since it means that the reader only gradually learns, through certain internal evidence, that Sister is specifically located outside her home. The gradualness of the revelation permits the reader to appreciate first, the vividness of her past before coming to see the pale reality of her present condition which she poignantly tries to glamorize for the listener and for herself.

It is important for the stage designer to avoid identifying the downstage right area too specifically with the "P.O." Let the area be generalized as a place which is merely peripheral to the main action which is stage center.

There are, of course, subtle references throughout the early scenes to a place and a time that are *here* and *now* rather than *there* and *then*. These references gradually prepare the listener for his role of confidant in the "P.O." at the conclusion of the story. If there should be further need for justifying Sister's presence in the "P.O." throughout the story, look to the title, "Why I Live at the P.O." The present tense of the verb in the title is a strong indication that Sister, the "I" of the title, is living at *present* in the "P.O."

* * *

Considerations of time and place are seldom matters of indifference to an author in the act of creating a story, and they should be matters of no less importance to the reader as interpreter of the story. The very nature of Chamber Theatre, with its insistence on specifications of time and place, compels the audience to be concerned with such matters and, to that extent, reveals the inner structure of narrative fiction.

It is sometimes argued that staging fiction is a distortion of the author's intention, which surely involved a reading rather than an observing public. It is not surprising to find that in general people are content to enjoy reading fiction silently while preferring to go to the theatre to see plays. Nonetheless, increasing sales of the printed texts of plays seem to indicate that the public is learning to take pleasure in reading plays silently, and one wonders if the converse might not also be true, if there might not be a market for fiction performed on the stage. That it has not been done is not to argue that it cannot or should not be done. The structural similarities of modern drama and modern fiction suggest that the two genres might share the same environment. It is conceivable that if the drama, whose natural habitat is the theatre, is not without honor in the library, then, the novel or short story, already at home in the library, might be welcome on the stage.

Furthermore, there is no obligation on the part of the interpreter to respect the author's intentions. Once the story is made, the reader looks to *it* for meaning, not to the author's intentions; he or she is responsible to the text, not to the author. If a reader finds that the quality of a particular fiction can be understood best in a Chamber Theatre production, then the stage becomes, for that person, a satisfactory environment for the work.

The interpreter's perception of the meaning of any work of art is not a series of static impressions received from a complex of stable patterns, but rather "an invasion of the organism by external forces which upset the balance of the nervous system."[16] The proper understanding of a work of fiction depends upon the balancing of antagonistic forces, those of the invading text and those of the resistant interpreter.

These forces have their freest play, perhaps, on the stage in a Chamber Theatre production where the director and the performers actively engage the vital forces of fiction.

The carrier of fictional values in a Chamber Theatre production is a "continously existing object";[17] actors in motion, characters in action are experienced by the spectator as an "object of immediate perception." Under the direction of the narrator, the behavior of the actors creates an intricate pattern of interacting characters which forms the basis of the audience's evaluation of the novel or short story as an "object of criticism."

If Chamber Theatre facilitates the viewer's evaluation of fiction as an object of criticism, no further justification of the technique is necessary.

---

[16]Rudolf Arnheim, *Art and Visual Perception*, p. 398. Copyright © 1954 & 1974 by the Regents of the University of California; reprinted by permission of the University of California Press.

[17]Stephen C. Pepper, *The Work of Art* (Bloomington: Indiana University Press, 1955). See Chapter One for a fuller discussion of the nature and structure of an aesthetic object.

BIBLIOGRAPHY

CHAPTER 1

MORRIS, CHARLES W. *Signs, Language and Behavior*. New York: George Braziller. 1959.

———. "Foundations of a Theory of Signs." *International Encyclopedia of Unified Science*, Vol. 1. No. 2. University of Chicago Press, 1938.

CHAPTER 2

AUDEN, W. H. "Hic et Ille." In *The Dyer's Hand*. New York: Random House, 1962.

BACON, WALLACE A., AND ROBERT S. BREEN. *Literature as Experience*. New York: McGraw-Hill, 1959.

BERNE, ERIC. *Transactional Analysis in Psychotherapy*. New York: Grove Press, Inc., 1961.

CASSIRER, ERNST. *An Essay on Man*. New York: Doubleday Anchor Books, 1953.

———. *The Philosophy of Symbolic Forms*. Vol. 1. Language. New Haven: Yale University, 1953.

DEMAN, PAUL. *Blindness and Insight: Essays in the Rhetoric of Contemporary Criticism*. New York: Oxford University Press, 1971. See especially Chapter III and VI.

DOSTOYEVSKY, FYODOR. *The Double*. Bloomington: Indiana University Press, 1958.

GASSET, JOSE, ORTEGA, Y. *The Dehumanization of Art*. Garden City, New York: Doubleday & Co., 1956. See "The Self and the Other" pp. 161-187.

GOFFMAN, ERVING. *The Presentation of the Self in Everyday Life*. New York: Doubleday Anchor Books, Doubleday & Co., 1959.

HASSAN, IHAB. *Radical Innocence: The Contemporary American Novel.* Princeton, New Jersey: Princeton University Press, 1961. See Part 1, Chapter 1, "The Modern Self in Recoil," pp. 11-33.

HEIDER, FRITZ. *The Psychology of Interpersonal Relations.* New York: John Wiley & Sons, Inc., 1958.

ISHERWOOD, CHRISTOPHER. *Down There on a Visit.* New York: Simon & Schuster, 1962.

JAMES, WILLIAM. *Psychology.* Cleveland: The World Publishing Co., 1948.

JUNG, CARL G. *Two Essays on Analytical Psychology.* London: Routledge & Kegan Paul, 1953.

KLUCKHOHN, CLYDE, AND HENRY A. MURRAY, EDS. *Personality in Nature, Society, and Culture.* New York: Alfred A. Knopf, 1949.

KOESTLER, ARTHUR. *Darkness at Noon.* New York: Modern Library, 1941.

———. *Darkness at Noon.* New York: Macmillan, 1941.

KUMAR, SHIV K., AND KEITH McKEAN. *Critical Approaches to Fiction.* New York: McGraw-Hill, 1968. See Part Seven pp. 267-392.

LAING, R. D. *The Divided Self.* New York: Pantheon Books, 1969.

———. *Self and Others.* New York: Pantheon Books, 1969.

LIDZ, THEODORE. *The Person: His Development Throughout the Life Cycle.* New York: Basic Books, Inc., 1968.

MACMURRAY, JOHN. *The Self as Agent.* New York: Harper & Brothers Publishers, 1957.

MATSON, FLOYD W. AND ASHLEY, MONTAGE, EDS. *The Human Dialogue.* New York: The Free Press, 1967.

MEAD, GEORGE H. *Mind, Self and Society.* Chicago: The University of Chicago Press, 1934.

MERLEAU-PONTY, MAURICE. *The Structure of Behavior.* Boston: Beacon Press, 1963.

MOEN, PETER. *Peter Moen's Diary.* New York: Creative Age Press, 1951.

MULLER, HERBERT J. *Science and Criticism.* New York: George Braziller, 1956.

MURPHY, GARDNER. *Personality: A Biosocial Approach to Origins and Structure.* New York: Harper & Brothers Publishers, 1947.

PERLS, FRITZ. *The Gestalt Approach & Eye Witness to Therapy.* New York: Bantam Books, Inc., 1976.

PERLS, FRITZ; RALPH F. HEFFERLINE,; AND PAUL GOODMAN, *Gestalt Therapy: Excitement and Growth in the Human Personality.* New York: The Julian Press, Inc., 1951.

"Perspectives on the Novel." In *Daedalus: Journal of the American Academy of Arts and Sciences* 92, no. 2 (1963) Cambridge, Mass.: Harvard University.

PFUETZE, PAUL E. *The Social Self.* New York: Bookman Associates, 1954.

PORTER, KATHERINE ANN. "Flowering Judas." Short Story Masterpieces. Edited by Robert Penn Warren and Albert Erskine. New York: Dell Publishing Company, 1954.

———. *Flowering Judas and Other Stories.* New York: Harcourt Brace Jovanovich, 1955.

ROGERS, CARL R. *On Becoming a Person.* Sentry Edition. Boston: Houghton Mifflin Co., 1961.

ROGERS, ROBERT. *A Psychoanalytic Study of the Double in Literature.* Detroit: Wayne State University Press, 1970.

SCHILDER, PAUL. *The Image and Appearance of the Human Body.* New York: International Universities Press, 1950.

STRAUSS, ANSELM L. *Mirrors and Masks: The Search for Identity.* Glencoe, Illinois: The Free Press of Glencoe, 1959.

SYMONDS, PERCIVAL M. *The Ego and the Self.* New York: Appleton-Century-Crofts, Inc., 1951.

VICKERY, OLGA W. *The Novels of William Faulkner.* Baton Rouge: Louisiana State University Press, 1959.

WOLFF, WERNER. *The Expression of Personality.* New York: Harper & Brothers, Publishers, 1943.

WOOLF, VIRGINIA. "Evening Over Essex: Reflections in a Motor Car." In *The Death of the Moth.* New York: Harcourt, Brace, 1942.

CHAPTER 3

ALDRIDGE, JOHN W., ED. *Critiques and Essays on Modern Fiction.* New York: The Ronald Press Co., 1952.

AUERBACH, ERICH. *Mimesis:* The Representation of Reality in Western Literature. Garden City, N.Y.: Doubleday & Co., 1953. See Chapter 20—"The Brown Stocking," pp. 463-488, for a discussion of "point of view" in Virginia Woolf's *To the Lighthouse.*

BARTH, JOHN. *End of the Road.* rev. ed. New York: Doubleday & Co., 1967.

BOOTH, WAYNE C. *The Rhetoric of Fiction.* Chicago, Illinois: The University of Chicago Press, 1961.

CAPOTE, TRUMAN. *Breakfast at Tiffany's.* New York: Random House, 1958.

———. *Breakfast at Tiffany's* from *Selected Writings of Truman Capote.* New York: Random House, 1958.

COPPARD, A. E. "The Third Prize." In *Short Story Masterpieces.* Edited by Robert Penn Warren and Albert Erskine. New York: Dell Publishing Co., 1954.

———. "The Third Prize." From *Collected Tales of A. E. Coppard.* New York: Alfred A. Knopf, 1951.

DAVIS, ROBERT MURRAY, ED. *The Novel: Modern Essays in Criticism.* Englewood Cliffs, N.J.: Prentice-Hall, 1969.

DONLEAVY, J. P. *The Ginger Man.* New York: Berkley Medallion Books, 1965.

EDEL, LEON. *The Psychological Novel: 1900-1950.* New York: J. B. Lippincott Co., 1955.

FAULKNER, WILLIAM. "Barn Burning." In *Short Story Masterpieces.* Edited by Robert Penn Warren and Albert Erskine. New York: Dell Publishing Co., 1954.

———. "Barn Burning." In *Collected Stories of William Faulkner.* New York: Random House, Inc., 1956.

FITZGERALD, F. SCOTT. *The Great Gatsby.* Reprinted from *The Portable F. Scott Fitzgerald.* New York: Viking Press, 1945.

FORSTER, E. M. *Aspects of the Novel.* Harcourt, Brace and Company, 1927.

GASS, WILLIAM H. *Fiction and the Figures of Life.* New York: Vintage Books, a division of Random House, 1972.

GASSET, JOSE ORTEGA Y. *The Dehumanization of Art.* Garden City, N.Y.: Doubleday & Co., 1956.

GOLDKNOPF, DAVID. *The Life of the Novel.* Chicago, Ill.: The University of Chicago Press, 1972.

GRASS, GÜNTER. *The Tin Drum.* Translated by Ralph Manheim. New York: Pantheon Books, 1961, 1962.

GROSSVOGEL, DAVID I. *Limits of the Novel.* Ithaca, N.Y.: Cornell University Press, 1968.

HARVEY, W. J. *Character and the Novel.* Ithaca, N.Y.: Cornell University Press, 1965.

HUGO, HOWARD E. *Aspects of Fiction: A Handbook.* Boston: Little, Brown and Co., 1962.

HUMPHREY, ROBERT. *Stream of Consciousness in the Modern Novel.* Berkeley and Los Angeles: University of California Press, 1954.

JAMES, HENRY. *The Art of Fiction: And Other Essays.* New York: Oxford University Press, 1948.

————. *The Art of the Novel: Critical Prefaces.* New York: Charles Scribner's Sons, 1950.

————. *Washington Square.* Reprinted in *Great American Short Novels.* Edited by William Phillips. New York: Dial Press, 1946.

JOYCE, JAMES. "Boarding House." In *Short Story Masterpieces.* Edited by Robert Penn Warren and Albert Erskine. New York: Dell Publishing Co., 1954.

KUMAR, SHIV K., AND MCKEAN, KEITH. *Critical Approaches to Fiction.* New York: McGraw-Hill Book Co., 1968.

LUBBOCK, PERCY. *The Craft of Fiction.* New York: Peter Smith, 1947.

MELVILLE, HERMAN. "Benito Cereno." In *The House of Fiction.* Edited by Caroline Gordon and Allen Tate. New York: Charles Scribner's Sons, 1950.

MUIR, EDWIN. *The Structure of the Novel.* New York: Harcourt, Brace and World, n.d.

NABOKOV, VLADIMIR. *Lolita.* New York: G. P. Putnam's Sons, 1955.

O'CONNOR, WILLIAM VAN, ED. *Forms of Modern Fiction.* Minneapolis, Minn.: The University of Minnesota Press, 1948.

PEARCE, ROY HARVEY, ED. *Experience in the Novel:* Selected Papers from the English Institute. New York: Columbia University Press, 1968.

"Perspectives on the Novel." In *Daedalus:* Journal of the American Academy of Arts and Sciences 92, no. 2 (1963) Cambridge, Mass.: Harvard University.

RABAN, JONATHAN. *The Technique of Modern Fiction: Essays in Practical Criticism.* Notre Dame, Indiana: University of Notre Dame Press, 1969.

ROMBERG, BERTIL. *Studies in the Narrative Technique of the First-Person Novel.* Stockholm: Almkvist and Wiksell, 1962.

SCHOLES, ROBERT. *Elements of Fiction.* New York: Oxford University Press, 1968.

————. *The Fabulators.* New York: Oxford University Press, 1967.

SCHOLES, ROBERT AND ROBERT KELLOGG. *The Nature of Narrative.* New York: Oxford University Press, 1966.

SOUVAGE, JACQUES. *An Introduction to the Study of the Novel.* Ghent: Wetenschappelijke Uitgeverij, E. Story- Scientia P.V.B.A., 1965.

STANZEL, FRANZ. *Narrative Situations in the Novel.* Bloomington, Indiana: Indiana University Press, 1971.

SURMELIAN, LEON. *Techniques of Fiction Writing: Measure and Madness.* Garden City, N. Y.: Doubleday and Co., 1968.

V AN GHENT, DOROTHY. *The English Novel.* New York: Harper & Row, Publishers, 1953.

WRIGHT, ANDREW H. *Jane Austen's Novels.* New York: Oxford University Press, 1954.

WRIGHT, GEORGE T. *The Poet in the Poem.* Berkeley and Los Angeles: University of California Press, 1962. See "The Faces of the Poet," p. 1.

CHAPTER 4

ALGREN, NELSON. "A Bottle of Milk for Mother." In *Short Story Masterpieces.* Edited by Robert Penn Warren and Albert Erskine. New York: Dell Publishing Co., 1954.

———. "A Bottle of Milk for Mother." From *The Neon Wilderness.* Magnolia, Mass.: Peter Smith Publishers, Inc., 1960.

BABB, HOWARD S., ED. *Essays in Stylistic Analysis.* New York: Harcourt Brace Jovanovich, Inc., 1972.

BARTHES, ROLAND. *Critical Essays.* Translated by Richard Howard. Evanston, Ill.: Northwestern University Press, 1972.

BROWN, HUNTINGTON. *Prose Styles: Five Primary Types.* Minneapolis, Minn.: The University of Minnesota Press, 1966.

CHATMAN, SEYMOUR, AND SAMUEL R., LEVIN., eds. *Essays on the Language of Literature.* Boston: Houghton Mifflin, 1967.

CHATMAN, SEYMOUR, ED. *Literary Style: A Symposium.* New York: Oxford University Press, 1971.

CULLER, JONATHAN. *Structuralist Poetics: Structuralism, Linguistics and the Study of Literature.* London: Routledge and Kegan Paul, 1975.

CUNNINGHAM, J. V., ED. *The Problem of Style.* Greenwich, Conn.: Fawcett Publications, Inc., 1966.

DAVIS, ROBERT MURRAY, ED. The Novel: Modern Essays in Criticism, pp. 254-265. Englewood Cliffs, N. J.: Prentice-Hall, Inc., 1969.

DOBRÉE, BONAMY. *Modern Prose Style.* Oxford: At the Clarendon Press, 1934.

English: Selected Readings and Exercises, Volume III, Twelfth Edition, February 1948. Chicago, Ill.: The University of Chicago Press.

FOWLER, ROGER, ED. *Essays on Style and Language: Linguistic and Critical Approaches to Literary Style.* London: Routledge and Kegan Paul, 1966.

———. *The Languages of Literature: Some Linguistic Contributions to Criticism.* London: Routledge and Kegan Paul, 1971.

HOLLAND, NORMAN N. *The Dynamics of Literary Response.* New York: Oxford University Press, 1968 See Chapter 8, "Style and the Man," pp. 225-242.

JACOBS, RODERICK A. AND PETER S. ROSENBAUM. *Transformations, Style, and Meaning.* Waltham, Mass.: Xerox College Publishing, 1971.

LANHAM, RICHARD A. *Style: An Anti-Texbook.* New Haven: Yale University Press, 1974.

MELVILLE, HERMAN. *Moby-Dick.* Edited by Harrison Hayford and Hershal Parker. New York: W. W. Norton, 1967.

MILIC, LOUIS T. *Stylists on Style: A Handbook with Selections for Analysis.* New York: Charles Scribner's Sons, Inc., 1969.

MURRY, JOHN MIDDLETON. *The Problem of Style*. London: Oxford University Press, first published 1922, first issued in Oxford Paperbacks, 1960.

O. HENRY. "The Furnished Room." in *The Four Million*. New York: Doubleday, 1912.

PECKHAM, MORSE. *Man's Rage for Order: Biology, Behavior, and the Arts*. New York: Schocken Books, 1967.

RABAN, JONATHAN. *The Technique of Modern Fiction: Essays in Practical Criticism*. Notre Dame, Indiana: University of Notre Dame Press, 1969.

READ, HERBERT. *English Prose Style*. London: G. Bell & Sons, Ltd., 1949.

SEBEOK, THOMAS, ED. *Style in Language*. New York: John Wiley & Sons, Inc. and The Technology Press of Massachusetts Institute of Technology, 1960.

SONTAG, SUSAN. *Against Interpretation*. Dell Publishing Co., 1966. See her essay, "On Style" pp. 15-36.

SPITZER, LEO. *Linguistics and Literary History*. Princeton: Princeton University Press, 1948.

SYPHER, WYLIE. *Four Stages of Renaissance Style: Transformations in Art and Literature 1400-1700*. Garden City, N. Y.: Doubleday & Co., 1955.

———. *Rococo to Cubism in Art and Literature: Transformations in Style, In Art and Literature from the 18th to the 20th Century*. New York: Vintage Books, a division of Random House, 1963.

WARREN, AUSTIN. *Rage for Order: Essays in Criticism*. Chicago: University of Chicago Press, 1948.

WELLEK, RENE AND AUSTIN, WARREN. *Theory of Literature*. New York: Harcourt Brace and World, Inc., 1949.

WHITEHEAD, ALFRED NORTH. *The Aims of Education and Other Essays*. New York: Mentor Books, 1949.

WILKINSON, A. M. "The State of Language." *Educational Review*, Vol. 22, No. 1, November 1969.

CHAPTER 5

ABEL, LIONEL. *Metatheatre: A New View of Dramatic Form*. New York: Hill and Wang, 1963.

BACON, WALLACE A. *The Art of Interpretation*. New York: Holt, Rinehart and Winston, 1972.

BENTLEY, ERIC. *In Search of Theatre*. New York: Vintage Books. Reprinted by arrangement with Alfred A. Knopf, 1954.

———. *The Playwright as Thinker: A study of the Modern Theatre*. New York: Meridian Books, published by The Noonday Press, 1955.

BOLT, ROBERT. *A Man for All Seasons*. London: Heinemann Educational Books Ltd., 1968.

BRECHT, BERTOLT. "A Little Organum for the Theatre." *Accent*, Winter, 1951.

———. "A New Technique of Acting." Translated by Eric Bentley. *Theatre Arts*, 33 No. 1 (January 1949).

"Bertolt Brecht." *The Drama Review* (TDR) Vol. 12, No. 1 (T37) Fall 1967.

"The Theatre of Bertolt Brecht." *The Tulane Drama Review*. New Orleans: Tulane University, Vol. 6, No. 1, September 1961.

BRUSTEIN, ROBERT. *The Theatre of Revolt: An Approach to the Modern Drama.* Boston: Little Brown & Co., 1964.

BUDEL, OSCAR. "Contemporary Theatre and Aesthetic Distance." In Brecht: *A Collection of Critical Essays.* Edited by Peter Demetz, Englewood Cliffs, N. J., Prentice-Hall, Inc., 1962.

BULLOUGH, EDWARD. "Psychical Distance as a Factor in Art and an Aesthetic Principle." *British Journal of Psychology,* 5 (1912), 87-98.

COLE, TOBY AND HELEN KRICH CHINOY, EDS. *Actors and Acting.* New York: Crown Publishers, 1949. See "Bertolt Brecht," pp. 280-285. Also "Erwin Piscator," pp. 285-291.

———. *Directors on Directing.* Indianapolis: The Bobbs-Merrill Co., 1963. See Bertolt Brecht, "A Model for Epic Theater," pp. 234-244. Also Bertolt Brecht, Model for *Mother Courage and Her Children,* Scenes XI and XII, pp. 333-346. And "The Use of the Epic Model," pp. 347-350.

DUNCAN, HUGH DALZIEL. *Language and Literature in Society.* Chicago: The University of Chicago Press, 1953.

ESSLIN, MARTIN. *The Theatre of the Absurd.* Garden City, N.Y.: Doubleday & Co., 1961.

HOLTHUSEN, HANS EGON. "Brecht's Dramatic Theory." In *Brecht: A Collection of Critical Essays.* Edited by Peter Demetz. Englewood Cliffs, N. J.: Prentice-Hall, Inc., 1962.

JOYCE, JAMES. *Portrait of the Artist as a Young Man.* New York: The Modern Library, 1928.

MUNK, ERIKA, ED. *Brecht.* New York: Bantam Books, 1972.

PRONKO, LEONARD C. *Theater East and West: Perspectives Toward a Total Theatre.* Berkeley and Los Angeles: University of California Press, 1967.

SALINGER, J. D. *Franny and Zooey.* Boston: Little, Brown, 1961.

STRAUS, ERWIN W., AND RICHARD M. GRIFFITH., EDS. *Phenomenology of Will and Action: The Second Lexington Conference on Pure and Applied Phenomenology.* Pittsburgh, Pa.: Duquesne University Press, 1967.

WILLETT, JOHN, ED. *Brecht on Theatre: The Development of an Aesthetic.* New York: Hill and Wang, 1964.

———. *The Theatre of Bertolt Brecht:* A Study from Eight Aspects. Norfolk, Conn.: New Directions Books, 1959.

CHAPTER 6

ARNHEIM, RUDOLF. *Film as Art.* Berkeley and Los Angeles: University of California Press, 1957.

BAZIN, ANDRE. *What is Cinema?* Berkeley and Los Angeles: University of California Press, 1967.

BERGMAN, INGMAR. "Introduction." *Four Screenplays of Ingmar Bergman.* New York: Simon & Schuster, 1960.

BLUESTONE, GEORGE. *Novels into Film.* Baltimore: Johns Hopkins Press, 1957.

BOBKER, LEE R. *Elements of Film.* New York: Harcourt, Brace & World, 1969.

EDEL, LEON. "Novel and Camera." In *The Theory of the Novel: New Essays,* pp. 177-188. Edited by John Halperin. New York: Oxford University Press, 1974.

FELL, JOHN L. *Film and the Narrative Tradition.* Norman: University of Oklahoma Press, 1974.

FLAUBERT, GUSTAVE. *Madame Bovary.* New York: Random House, The Modern Library, n.d. For a Fuller discussion of crosscutting in literature see *Film Form* pp. 10 ff. by Sergei Bisenstein. New York: Harcourt Brace, 1949.

GEDULD, HARRY M., ED. *Film Makers on Film Making.* Bloomington, Ind.: Indiana University Press, 1969.

GESSNER, ROBERT. "The Film: A Source of New Vitality for the Novel." Book Review Section. *New York Times,* 7 August 1960.

———. *The Moving Image: A Guide to Cinematic Literacy.* New York: E. P. Dutton, 1970.

HEMINGWAY, ERNEST. "Cat in the Rain." From *In Our Time* by Ernest Hemingway. New York: Charles Scribner's Sons, 1925, 1930.

HUME, DAVID. *A Treatise of Human Nature,* Book I, Part I, Section 1. London: Oxford University Press

HUSS, ROY AND NORMAN SILVERSTEIN. *The Film Experience.* New York: Dell Publishing Co., Inc., 1968.

JACOBS, LEWIS, ED. *The Movies as Medium.* New York: Farrar, Straus & Giroux, 1970.

KAWIN, BRUCE F. *Tell It Again and Again: Repetition in Literature and Film.* Ithaca: Cornell University Press, 1972.

KRACAUER, SIEGFRIED. *Theory of Film: The Redemption of Physical Reality.* New York: Oxford University Press, 1965.

LANGER, SUSANNE. *Problems of Art.* New York: Charles Scribner's Sons, 1957.

LAWRENCE, D. H. "The Horse Dealer's Daughter." In *Short Story Masterpieces.* Edited by Robert Penn Warren and Albert Erskine. New York: Dell Publishing Co., 1954.

———. "The Horse Dealer's Daughter." From *The Complete Short Stories of D.H. Lawrence.* Viking Press and Mrs. Frieda Lawrence, 1961.

LAWSON, JOHN HOWARD. *Film: The Creative Process, The Search for an Audio-Visual Language and Structure.* 2d ed. New York: Hill and Wang, 1967.

LEVIN, HARRY. *James Joyce: A Critical Introduction.* Norfolk, Conn.: New Directions Books, 1941.

LINDGREN, ERNEST. *The Art of the Film: An Introduction to Film Appreciation.* London: George Allen and Unwin, Ltd., 1948.

MACCANN, RICHARD DYER. *Film: A Montage of Theories.* New York: E. P. Dutton, 1966.

MILLER, TONY AND PATRICIA GEORGE MILLER. *"Cut! Print!: The Language and Structure of Filmmaking.* New York: Da Capo Press, Inc., 1975.

MONTAGU, IVOR. *Film World: A Guide to Cinema.* Baltimore, Md.: Penguin Books, 1964.

MUNSTERBERG, HUGO. *The Film: A Psychological Study.* New York: Dover Publications, Inc., 1970.

PERKINS, V. F. *Film as Film: Understanding and Judging Movies.* Harmondsworth, Middlesex, England: Penguin Books Ltd., 1972.

P᷉UDOVKIN, V. I. *Film Technique and Film Acting.* Edited and translated by Ivor Montagu. New York: Grove Press, Inc., 1960.

R᷉EAD, HERBERT. "The Poet and the Film." In *A Coat of Many Colors.* London: George Routledge & Sons, Ltd., 1947.

R᷉ICHARDSON, ROBERT. *Literature and Film.* Bloomington, Ind.: Indiana University Press, 1969.

R᷉OBBE-GRILLET, ALAIN. *Jealousy.* In *Two Novels by Robbe-Grillet, Jealousy and In the Labyrinth.* New York: Grove Press, Inc., 1965.

———. *Last Year at Marienbad.* New York: Grove Press, Inc., 1962.

R᷉USSELL, BERTRAND. *Analysis of Mind.* London: George Allen and Unwin, Ltd., 1949.

S᷉POTTISWOODE, RAYMOND. *A Grammar of the Film: An Analysis of Film Technique.* Berkeley and Los Angeles: University of California Press, 1951.

S᷉TEPHENSON, RALPH AND DEBRIX, JEAN R. *The Cinema as Art.* Baltimore, Md.: Penguin Books Inc., 1965.

T᷉EMANER, GERALD. "Toward an Aesthetic of the Film." *New University Thought.* Spring, 1961.

T᷉UDOR, ANDREW. *Theories of Film.* New York: Viking Press, 1974.

T᷉YLER, PARKER. *The Shadow of an Airplane Climbs the Empire State Building: A World Theory of Film.* Garden City, N. Y.: Anchor Press/Doubleday, 1973.

W᷉OLLEN, PETER. *Signs and Meaning in the Cinema.* Bloomington, Ind.: Indiana University Press, 1969.

Y᷉OUNGBLOOD, GENE. *Expanded Cinema.* N. Y.: E. P. Dutton, 1970.

CHAPTER 7

B᷉RECHT, BERTOLT. "Der Buhnenbau des Epischen Theatres." Reprinted in an English translation in *World Theatre,* 4, No. 1—*The Actor* (Winter, 1954).

C᷉OPPARD, A. E. "Fifty Pounds." From *The Collected Tales of A. E. Coppard.* New York: Alfred A. Knopf, 1948.

L᷉AWRENCE, D. H. "The Fox." In *Short Novels of the Masters.* Edited by Charles Neider. New York: Rinehart & Co., 1948.

———. *The Fox.* From *The Portable D. H. Lawrence.* New York: Viking Press, 1947.

O'C᷉ONNOR, FRANK. "My Oedipus Complex." In *Short Story Masterpieces.* Edited by Robert Penn Warren and Albert Erskine. New York: Dell Publishing Co., 1954.

———. "My Oedipus Complex." From *The Stories of Frank O'Connor.* New York: Alfred A. Knopf, 1952.

P᷉OWERS, J. F. "The Valiant Woman." In *Short Story Masterpieces.* Edited by Robert Penn Warren and Albert Erskine. New York: Dell Publishing Co., 1954.

———. "The Valiant Woman." From *Prince of Darkness.* Garden City, New York: Doubleday, 1948.

R᷉OTH, PHILIP. *Portnoy's Complaint.* New York: Bantam Books, 1970.

S᷉TAFFORD, JEAN. "A Country Love Story." In *Short Story Masterpieces.* Edited by Robert Penn Warren and Albert Erskine. New York: Dell Publishing Co., 1954.

————. "A Country Love Story." From *Children Are Bored on Sunday*. New York: Harcourt Brace, 1953.

TYNAN, KENNETH. Report of a visit to the *Theater an Schiffbauerdamn* in East Berlin. Printed in Perspective, June, 1962, p. 32.

CHAPTER 8

AIKEN, CONRAD. "Impulse." In *Short Story Masterpieces*. Edited by Robert Penn Warren and Albert Erskine. New York: Dell Publishing Co., 1954.

————. "Impulse." In *Short Stories of Conrad Aiken*. New York: Hawthorne Books, Inc., 1950.

ARNHEIM, RUDOLF. *Art and Visual Perception*. Berkeley and Los Angeles: University of California Press, 1965.

CRANE, STEPHEN. "The Bride Comes to Yellow Sky." In *Short Story Masterpieces*. New York: Dell Publishing Co., 1954.

————. "The Bride Comes to Yellow Sky." From *The Work of Stephen Crane*. Edited by Wilson Follett. New York: Alfred A. Knopf, 1926. Vol. XII.

PEPPER, STEPHEN C. *The Work of Art*. Bloomington: Indiana University Press, 1955. See Chapter One for a fuller discussion of the nature and structure of an aesthetic object.

WELTY, EUDORA. "Why I Live at the P.O." In *Short Story Masterpieces*. New York: Dell Publishing Co., 1954.

————. "Why I Live at the P.O." From *A Curtain of Green*. New York: Harcourt Brace, 1946.

INDEX

Acting, objective, 43
Actor/Actress, 42-43, 45, 49-51, 69, 70-71
  behavior in Chamber Theatre, 69
  of Berliner Ensemble, 70-71
  and Chamber Theatre, 71
  as demonstrator, 42-43, 45
  and double-distance, 49-51
  Piscator and Epic acting, 69
  in theatre, 45
Aesthetic distance, 48, 50-51
  definition of, 48
  epiphanal nature of, 48
  increased and decreased, 50-51
  and narrator, 50
Aesthetic experience, 48-49
  as double-distance, 48
  as epiphany, 48-49
Aiken, Conrad, 13, 90
Albee, Edward, 5
Algren, Nelson, 36, 46-47
Alienation-effect, 43-46, 73-75
  and Chamber Theatre, 44
  and character-actor relation, 75
  and Epic Theatre, 43-44
  and narration, 73-74
  paradox of (Bolt), 45
  paradox of (Brecht), 46
Angle of vision (see Point of view)
Anna Karenina, 4, 10, 87
Antony & Cleopatra, 3, 77
Arsenic and Old Lace, 49

Auden, W.H., 17
Audience, 54
  in Chamber Theatre, 54
  in legitimate and movie theatre, 54
Author's intentions, 114

Bacon, Wallace A., 13
Ballad of the Sad Cafe, 42
"Barn Burning," 28-30
Barth, John, 5, 24
Bazin, André, 56
Beckett, Samuel, 6
Benito Cereno, 60
Bergman, Ingmar, 57-58
"Boarding House, The," 30-31
Bolt, Robert, 43
Booth, Wayne C., 33-34
"Bottle of Milk for Mother, A," 36-37,
    46-47
Bowen, Elizabeth, 10
Boys from Syracuse, The, 10
Breakfast at Tiffany's, 26-27
Brecht, Bertolt, 42, 69, 71, 79-80
"Bride Comes to Yellow Sky, The, 102-105
Budel, Oscar, 50-51
Bullough, Edward, 48

Capote, Truman, 26
"Cat in the Rain," 59

Caucasian Chalk Circle, The, 42
Chamber Theatre, 4-6, 11-13, 26-35, 37,
        39-40, 44, 56, 61, 63-68, 77-79,
        113
    angle of vision, 4 (see Point of view)
    alienation effects in performance, 44
    author's biography irrelevant, 40
    definition of, 4
    distance, 44
    and dramatizing style, 39
    and film, 56
    filmic staging of "The Horse Dealer's
        Daughter," 63-66
    filmic staging of *Jealousy,* 66-68
    and flashbacks, 61
    function, 37
    and mirror, 11-13
    narrator and action in, 39
    and point of view, 34
    and settings, 77-79
    simultaneity and motivations, 4-5
    staging narrator as major character, 26
    staging narrator as minor character,
        27-28
    staging objective narrator, 32-33
    staging omniscient narrator, 29-31
    and structure of fiction, 113
    and style, 35
    symbolic action in literary text, 40
    as technique, 6
Comedy of Errors, The, 10
Conrad, Joseph, 2, 10
Coppard, A.E., 32, 97
Costumes, 80-82
    and character, 80
    consistency of, 82
    and narrator, 80, 82
    suggestive, 81
"Country Love Story, A," 106-8
Crane Stephen, 102

Darkness at Noon, 8
"Demon Lover, The," 10
Director, 49, 69-70, 85-87
    as adapter, 85-86
    choosing fiction, 86
    cutting the text, 87
    and double-distance, 49
    Piscator and Epic Theatre staging,
        69-70
"Doctor Jekyll and Mr. Hyde," 10
Donleavy, J.P., 24
Don Quixote, 4, 87
Dostoyevsky, Fyodor, 10, 14
Double, The, 10, 14-15
Double, 14-15
    autoscopic experiments, 15
    intracharacter conflict, 14

Double-distance, 48-53
    in Chamber Theatre, 53
    and director, 49
    in drama, 50-52
    in fiction, 52-53
    and narrator, 50
    object and aesthetic condition, 50
Down There on a Visit, 15-17
Drama, 2-5, 32, 42, 50-52, 77, 114
    and the confidant, 2
    double-distance, 50-52
    and narration, 42
    and narrative devices, 5
    and narrator, 42
    and objective narrator, 32
    and settings, 77
    simultaneity of action, 3-4
    soliloquy, 2
    structural similarities to fiction, 114
Dramatic mode, 2
    language of, 2
    showing a story, 2
Dramatist, 2-3
    show and tell, 2
    translating novel into play, 3
Duncan, Hugh Dalziel, 53

End Game, 42
End of the Road, 24
Epic literature (see Fiction)
Epic mode (see Narrative)
Epic situation, 21-23, 26-27, 31-32
    of narrator as major character, 21-23
    of narrator as minor character, 26-27
    of objective narrator, 31-32
Epic Theatre, 42-53
    alienation, 42
    "alienation effect," 43-44
    definition of, 42-43
    as Dialectic Theatre, 46
    paradox of alienation, 45
    Piscator and "objective acting," 43
    and Theater of Encounter, 47
    and Theatre of Involvement, 47
Epiphany, 48-50
    in art, 50
"Evening Over Essex: Reflections in a
        Motor Car," 20

Faulkner, William, 5, 12, 28
Fiction, 3, 46, 56, 58-64, 77
    and cinematic concepts, 58-64
    and crosscutting, 62-63
    and film, 56
    motivation, 3
    and settings, 77
    tensiveness in, 46

"Fifty Pounds," 74
Film, 54-68
    and Chamber Theatre, 56
    and crosscutting, 62
    and fiction, 56-57
    filmic staging of "The Horse Dealer's
        Daughter," 63-66
    filmic staging of *Jealousy,* 66-68
    images and language, 57
    literature and film (Bergman), 57-58
    literature and film (Gessner), 58-61
    literature and film (Read), 58
    and novel as narrative, 55
Film-makers, 54
    and novelist, 54
    and point of view, 54
Fitzgerald, F. Scott, 27
Flaubert, Gustave, 62-63
"Flowering Judas," 8-9
Fox, The, 76-77, 84-85
"Furnished Room, The," 37-39

"Garden Party, The," 10
Gessner, Robert, 58
Ghosts, 42
Ginger Man, The, 24-26
"Girl in the Mirror, The," 12
Glass Menagerie, The, 42, 50
Good Woman of Setzuan, The, 68-70
Grapes of Wrath, The, 78
Grass, Günter, 22
Great Gatsby, The, 27

Hand props, 82-85
    actual and imaginary, 83-84
    in staging *The Fox,* 84-85
Hemingway, Ernest, 59, 60-61, 86
Henry V, 42
"Horse Dealer's Daughter, The," 63-66
Hume, David, 57

"I" and "Me," 17-19
Iliad, The, 82
"Impulse," 13, 90-96
Isherwood, Christopher, 15

James, Henry, 30
James, William, 17-18
Jealousy, 66-68
Joyce, James, 5-6, 30, 49-50, 56
Jung, Carl G., 7
Justine, 10

Kafka, Franz, 6

"Killers, The," 86
Koestler, Arthur, 8

Langer, Susanne, 62
Last Year at Marienbad, 61
Lawrence, D.H., 63, 76, 84-85
Levin, Harry, 56
Light in August, 12
Lighting, 79-80
    Brecht and, 79-80
    relation of character and narrator, 79
    and mood, 79
Living Theatre, The, 47
Lolita, 23

Madame Bovary, 62-63
Man for All Seasons, A, 42
Mansfield, Katherine, 10
Marquis de Sade, 10
Mead, George H., 18
Medea, 42
Melville, Herman, 60
Menaechmi, The, 10
Merleau-Ponty, Maurice, 10-11
Moby-Dick, 4, 40-41, 87
Moen, Peter, 8
Mirror, 10-11, 13, 16, 70
    and alienation, 70
    and Chamber Theatre, 11
    as distortion, 13
    and the double, 10
    and memory, 16
    as metaphor, 13
Muller, Herbert J., 18
"My Oedipus Complex," 75

Nabokov, Vladimir, 6, 23
Narration, 35, 37, 42, 46, 72-75
    and actor/actress, 74-75
    and alienation, 73-74
    and identification, 46
    and staging, 72
    and storyteller, 42
    and style, 35, 37
Narrative, 2-3, 5, 33, 55-56, 75
    devices in drama, 5
    in film and novel, 55-56
    language of, 2
    lyric and dramatic elements, 33
    and narrator, 75
    telling a story, 2
    translation into dramatic mode, 3
Narrator, 21-34, 36-39, 46-47, 50, 55, 58,
        61, 72-77, 79-80
    aesthetic distance, 50
    as agent, 39

Narrator *(cont.)*
  as camera, 55, 58
  in Chamber Theatre, 55
  and character, 55
  costumes, 80
  diction, 38, 46
  diction as character, 36-37
  and double-distance, 50
  first-person major character, 21-26
    bifurcation, 26
    definition of, 21
    duality, 22
    point of view, 23-26
    staging, 26
  and flashbacks, 61
  identification, 46-47
  inflections and gestures, 39
  and lighting, 79
  as lyric element, 33
  first-person minor character, 26-28
    definition of, 26
    staging, 27-28
  naration, 34, 74
  point of view, 39
  simultaneous speech, 76-77
  staging, 72-73
    first-person, 72
    omniscient, 73
    third-person, 72-73
  style, 36
  third-person objective, 31-34
    definition of, 32
    as director, 33
    staging, 32-34
  third-person omniscient, 28-31
    as character, 31
    definition of, 28
    function of, 30
    qualified omniscience, 30
    staging, 29-31
  and time and space, 75-76
Novel, 4-5 (see also Fiction)
  "intransitive attention," 5
  serial representation of action, 4
Novelist, 2, 57
  and Hume, 57
  shows *and* tells a story, 2

O'Connor, Frank, 75
Odyssey, The, 82
O. Henry, 37
"Open Window, The," 87
Our Town, 42, 50-51

Picasso, Pablo, 12
Piscator, Erwin, 43, 69-70
Plato, 7

Point of view, 4, 21-34
  angle of vision, 4
  central intelligence, 33
  objective/subjective, 29
  value of Chamber Theatre presentation,
    34
Porter, Katherine Anne, 8
Preparation of text, 85-88
  choosing fiction, 86
  cutting text, 86-87
  director as adapter, 85-86

Read, Herbert, 58
Robbe-Grillet, Alain, 61, 66-67
Rogers, Robert, 14
Romberg, Bertil, 21
Russell, Bertrand, 57

"Saki," 87
Salinger, J.D., 52
Sample scripts, 89-114
  "Bride Comes to Yellow Sky, The,"
    102-5
  "Country Love Story, A," 105-8
  "Impulse," 90-96
  "Third Prize, The," 97-101
  "Why I Live at the P.O." 108-13
Sartre, Jean-Paul, 6
Scenery, 77-79
Schilder, Paul, 11-12, 19
Secret Sharer, The, 10
Self, 6-20
  dissociation of, 9
  as subject/object, 18
Self-knowledge, 6-8
  introspective monologues, 6-7
  in prison, 7-8
  psychic dialogues, 7
Selves as interactive characters, 19
Shakespeare, 3, 77
  narrative devices in his plays, 3
  and realism, 77
Show and tell, 1-3, 33
Socrates, 7
Spitzer, Leo, 39
Stafford, Jean, 106
Staging Chamber Theatre, 69-88
  costumes, 80-82
  handprops, 82-85
  lighting, 79-80
  preparation of the text, 85-88
  scenery, 77-79
Steinbeck, John, 78
Stevenson, R.L., 10
Strindberg, August, 4
  Chamber Plays, 4

Style, 35-41
    definition of, 35-36, 39
    and narration, 35
    narrator's point of view, 41
    stylistic analysis, 39
    written and spoken, 35

Temaner, Gerald, 55
Tensiveness, 43, 46
    between objectivity and subjectivity, 46
    definition of, 43
"Third Prize, The," 32, 97-101

Time, 61-62
Tin Drum, The, 22-23
Tom Jones, 82

"Valiant Woman, The," 88

Washington Square, 30
Welty, Eudora, 9, 87, 109
Whitehead, Alfred North, 36
"Why I Live at the P.O.," 87, 108-13
Wilder, Thornton, 5, 52
Williams, Tennessee, 5
Woolf, Virginia, 20